GROw
YOUR
OWN
FOOD

GROW YOUR OWN FOOD

CLARE MACNAUGHTON

White Owl
AN IMPRINT OF PEN & SWORD BOOKS LTD.
YORKSHIRE – PHILADELPHIA

First published in Great Britain in 2022 by
White Owl
An imprint of
Pen & Sword Books Ltd
Yorkshire - Philadelphia

Copyright © Clare Macnaughton, 2022

ISBN 978 1 39900 179 3

The right of Clare Macnaughton to be identified as author of this work has been asserted by her in accordance with the Copyright, Designs and Patents Act 1988.

A CIP catalogue record for this book is available from the British Library.

All rights reserved. No part of this book may be reproduced or transmitted in any form or by any means, electronic or mechanical including photocopying, recording or by any information storage and retrieval system, without permission from the Publisher in writing.

Typeset in 11/14 pts Cormorant Infant
by SJmagic DESIGN SERVICES, India.
Printed and bound by Short Run Press Limited, Exeter.

Pen & Sword Books Ltd incorporates the imprints of Pen & Sword Books Archaeology, Atlas, Aviation, Battleground, Discovery, Family History, History, Maritime, Military, Naval, Politics, Railways, Select, Transport, True Crime, Fiction, Frontline Books, Leo Cooper, Praetorian Press, Seaforth Publishing, Wharncliffe and White Owl.

For a complete list of Pen & Sword titles please contact

PEN & SWORD BOOKS LIMITED
47 Church Street, Barnsley, South Yorkshire, S70 2AS, England
E-mail: enquiries@pen-and-sword.co.uk
Website: www.pen-and-sword.co.uk

or

PEN AND SWORD BOOKS
1950 Lawrence Rd, Havertown, PA 19083, USA
E-mail: Uspen-and-sword@casematepublishers.com
Website: www.penandswordbooks.com

Contents

	About the Author	6
Chapter 1	From Pot to Patch	7
Chapter 2	The Seed of an Idea	25
Chapter 3	Propagation	30
Chapter 4	Seeing the Light	69
Chapter 5	Harvesting the Fruits of your Labour	91
Chapter 6	Foraging	104
Chapter 7	Keeping Chickens	109
	Index	120

About the Author

Clare Macnaughton lives in Wiltshire with her family. In 2010, she began to explore sustainable living and growing her own food, keeping pigs, sheep, chickens and ducks. Following the successful growth of some vegetables, and some less successfully, she has enjoyed and endured the hands-on experience of the ups and downs of animal husbandry and food growing. She has also grown two children, finding that vegetables are less complicated and don't answer back.

CHAPTER 1

From Pot to Patch

In 2020, before the UK was directed into lockdown, during the Coronavirus pandemic supermarkets were crammed with people panic-buying toilet roll; but instead I headed straight to my local garden centre and bought seeds, compost, pots, a windowsill propagator and a small pop up greenhouse in preparation for seed propagation so I could grow my own food. In addition to my vegetable garden accoutrements, I also bought a second-hand chicken house, three ex-battery hens for £4 each, a bag of straw, a bag of sawdust, layers pellets, corn feed, and created a bijou chicken area in small corner of the garden to ensure that I had a ready supply of eggs over the coming weeks.

The March 2020 UK Coronavirus lockdown had conveniently coincided with spring planting, which is also the perfect time to begin cultivating your own food. However, it's important to set expectations for your own success. It's not realistic to go from zero to professional gardener in a matter of minutes. Growing food takes time, care and patience.

I have been experimenting with growing vegetables, leaves and herbs over the last 10 years and I have had varying degrees of success, with some notable and amusing failures, including bunches of carrots looking like gnarled fingers, aubergines which have repeatedly foiled me, and baby sweetcorn with the texture of rope. Conversely, I have enjoyed great pleasure and satisfaction from harvesting my own potatoes, cooking them and serving them with butter, and freshly chopped chives, also from my garden. There is something wonderfully enriching about snipping herbs and leaves that you have grown and savouring the flavour in your daily victuals.

Water is a key element to grow your own food.

The basics of growth

In order to grow anything, you need soil, water and sunlight (around six to eight hours per day). Balancing the combination of these three elements is how different types of food are grown. The skill of how to grow abundantly relies on learning how to create the right conditions for the different types of food to thrive and grow.

How much space, time and energy do you have?

It's important to work out how much physical space you have to occupy your growing needs, how much time you have to manage and maintain the space, and how much physical energy you have to undertake the tasks needed to grow food successfully. The beauty of growing food is that it is scalable. It is entirely possible to grow manageable amounts of plants in pots on your windowsill, or, instead, if you have lots of space and energy, to work tirelessly on a homestead or smallholding.

Windowsill gardens

Growing plants on a windowsill is a practical and decorative solution to year-round gardening. You can pick a specific theme for your garden, or plant a variety of herbs and vegetables. If the windowsill doesn't provide the required six to eight hours of sun for vegetables, you may need to use a supplemental light source that provides full UV spectrum light, as well as situating your windowsill garden in a southern or eastern facing window. Be aware that a south facing windowsill in the summer can get too hot for most plants, so shading may be needed, or plants moved to a different windowsill. Herbs, vegetables and leaves can be grown in almost any kind of container that can drain (so it must have drainage holes in the bottom), and is loaded with rich soilless potting mix.

If your home is dry, you may need to create some humidity using a tray with pebbles and water, or by regularly misting plants. Be aware of insects that may attempt to make a home in your windowsill garden. However, a mix of washing up liquid and water sprayed liberally on the plants should minimise most pest invasions.

Windowsills are great for growing in pots.

Raised beds are a manageable way to grow a variety of vegetables.

Raised beds

Raising your garden beds can make growing fruit, vegetables and flowers easier, as it reduces the amount of time spent bending down. Raised beds can be constructed from anything that will hold soil and doesn't rot. There are many simple, safe and cheap ways to make raised beds using materials such as railway sleepers, used tyres, old wooden planks, old plastic buckets and even empty wooden pallets or crate boxes. The beds must be strong enough to hold the weight of the soil. The higher the bed the higher the risk of collapse so it's important to make sure that the bed is stable enough to contain the soil volume without falling over. Frozen soil expands, so if your outdoor space is susceptible to frost it's important to ensure the raised bed can accommodate this expansion. The raised bed needs to be able to drain the water away. Water can be drained through the wall of the raised beds by installing weep holes. Another advantage of raised beds is that they warm up quicker in the spring and are less compacted because they are not walked on. Make sure that you leave enough room between the beds to push your wheelbarrow through, otherwise the limited access can be frustrating.

Material ideas for raised beds

Used bricks and breeze blocks: They can make a good, cheap raised bed and also provide a seat to sit and garden from.

Sawn timber: This is a fairly low-cost material for making raised garden beds.

GROW YOUR OWN FOOD

Old planks: These can be assembled into a simple frame.

Buckets and containers: Potatoes grow well in old plastic buckets.

Old tyres: Two or three old tyres can be stacked on top of each other. They are good for growing vegetables as they absorb the heat in the day and radiate it off during the night, which helps the plants stay warm and encourages growth. To ensure stability and safety the stacked tyres should be held in place by hammered in stakes.

Railway sleepers: Robust and solid, sleepers look good, and when fixed sideways can form a seat to work from or rest. They are heavy to lift though, and can be expensive.

Softwood boards: Pressure-treated softwood boards fixed horizontally onto stakes driven into the ground make rustic, cost-effective raised beds. However, a bed made from softwood boards is not overly strong, so the maximum height of the bed should be around 450mm.

Pallet boxes or crates: Pre-constructed pallet boxes lined with weed matting and filled with top soil are easy-to-construct raised beds. The weed matting needs to be punctured around the walls in order to ensure adequate drainage.

I successfully created four pallet crate raised beds. I lined the pallet crates halfway with weed matting which I stapled to the edges. I ordered two tonnes of topsoil from a building supplier. I filled each crate with half a tonne of top soil and then punctured the weed matting around the sides for drainage purposes.

What is the perfect height, length and width of raised garden beds?

This is a bespoke scenario. Consider the position you will garden from, such as standing, kneeling or sitting next to, or on the edge of the bed. Hold a trowel in your dominant hand and reach out with your arm slightly lower than your shoulder. Measure the most comfortable position from the lowest point of the trowel to the ground. This is the optimum height for your raised bed. To determine the ideal width, measure the length of your arm, and the middle point of the bed should not be further than one arm's length reach away. The length of the bed is dependent on the space available. Make sure that you can work comfortably around the perimeter of the bed.

Allotments, patches, plots and polytunnels

When embarking on the transformation of your small site into a flourishing vegetable plot it is important to evaluate the state of play. Is it a blank canvas or have you inherited a plot? Does your plot have established fruit trees and crops? Regardless, of the state of your plot it is important to take your decisions carefully.

The first job is to clear away any weeds then turn over the soil. This can be done by hoeing, digging and raking.

Polytunnel

A polytunnel is large walk-in frame tunnel covered in plastic sheeting which prolongs the growing season.

What size of polytunnel do I need?

The size of polytunnel is dependent on how much space you have and what you intend to grow. You can select a polytunnel of any size, but it is worth noting that typical sizes for gardens and allotment plots range from widths of 2 to 5 metres and lengths of 2 to 20 metres. It is useful to have a minimum workable height at the centre of the tunnel of around 2 to 2.5 metres. The polytunnels tend to come in two basic designs: a semi-circular arc or a high tent shape. A well designed, constructed and maintained polytunnel can last for years.

Benefits of a polytunnel

- They absorb sunlight and so can achieve the most productive germination, and elevate spring growing temperatures two to six weeks prior to outdoor growing.
- Crops can grow faster, earlier and maybe larger.
- They are per square metre cheaper than glass or polycarbonate greenhouses.
- They are available in a wide range of sizes.

GROW YOUR OWN FOOD

Using polytunnels can prolong the growing season.

- They provide protection from destructive weather and therefore create ideal conditions for autumn, winter and early spring crops to be grown.
- It is possible to install irrigation systems using irrigation tubing with drip holes and set out different zones of small and large vegetables, soft fruits and tender fruit trees.

Considerations when buying a polytunnel
- Strength and durability of plastic sheeting cover.
- Ultraviolet resistance and how long the sheeting will last.
- The strength and quality of the metal framework.
- Ease of construction.
- Doors that can be easily sealed.
- The adaptability of the tunnel to help regulate the temperature so that it doesn't overheat, such as sides that open, shading that can be attached and available windbreak materials.
- They may not be permitted on all allotments, or there may be limits on how big the polytunnel can be.
- It should be air sealed at soil level to stop strong winds getting under the plastic and ballooning it.

Be warned that the use of insecticides and fungicides that are not ecological could create a toxic build-up and unsafe environment.

FROM POT TO PATCH

Polytunnels essentially provide shelter so you can harvest crops for longer and increase the variety of crops you can grow. The UK climate can be unpredictable and the weather can negatively impact crop growth.

A polytunnel provides a secure cover for your growing space. This means that both crops and gardener are well sheltered from the British weather, resulting in significantly improved working conditions.

Plant in the ground or put in pots in your polytunnel?
Growing crops in the open ground means your ground can then be improved year on year by adding organic matter. Most crops do grow best in a well-dug soil that is rich in organic material. Open ground holds moisture better than a pot and there is less need for growbag and compost. However, it's your polytunnel so grow what you like and in what you like. If you prefer pots then put your plants in pots. Do what makes you happy.

What can I grow in my polytunnel?
The polytunnel provides a suitable growing environment for most types of fruit or vegetable.

When do you want to harvest?
For an all year round yield then make sure there is enough space to sow your autumn and winter crop. Plan the space you have and allocated crop space in line with when they will harvest.

How much space do you have?
Think about how much room your crops will take up when they're growing. Do they spread out but yield little fruit, like a winter squash? Take some time to plan where you will plant and how expansive the plants are when fully grown.

Small field and vegetable patch

For the sake of debate, a small field will be considered as an acre or less. As with an allotment there are lots of things to consider with a field, but to some extent it's scalable. However, soil preparation and management is an essential part of successful vegetable growing. Good drainage is key because wet soil hinders vegetable growth. A sandy soil base has value as it drains more readily than the heavier soils. Well-drained soil is vital to the health of your crops and the yields you produce. Soil drainage can be accomplished by ditches and is more effective than other drainage methods, such as planting crops on ridges. Ditches remove excess water, but also enable essential air to penetrate the soil. Air is beneficial to soil organisms making nutrients available to the plants.

Turning over the soil by ploughing or rotavating destroys weeds and insects, and improves the soil texture and aeration. If crops are grown continuously then the soil can be sustained by ploughing annually. The soil depth for vegetables needs to be around a minimum of 15 to 20cm. On one level good soil management is an exercise in your own judgement. Your efforts should be centred on producing the desired crops with the optimum labour. It's important to consider soil erosion, the maintenance of soil organic matter and a planned, sustained crop rotation.

Soil erosion occurs as a result of water and wind. It is a hindrance when trying to grow vegetables because the topsoil is generally rich in fertile and organic matter. It is possible to control soil erosion with methods such as terracing, which divides the land into separate drainage areas, each with their own waterway above the terrace. Each terrace holds the water, which then soaks into the soil, thereby reducing, or even preventing, gullying.

A common method of crop planting is called contouring. This is when crops are planted across the field in rows at the same level. Cultivation then occurs along the rows instead of up and down the hill.

Strip cropping is a method of growing crops in narrow strips, across a slope, generally on a contour. Windbreaks can be used to prevent soil erosion by wind, coupled with feeding the soil with humus, as well as growing cover crops to retain the soil if no crops are planted. Humus is the organic element of soil, created by the decomposition of leaves and different plant materials by soil micro-organisms. It is essential that the organic matter content of the soil is maintained as it is the source of plant nutrients and plays an invaluable part in soil properties. Any loss of organic matter occurs due to the actions of micro-organisms which slowly decompose it down to carbon dioxide.

Adding manures and growing soil-improvement crops efficiently supply the soil with organic matter. The role of soil-improving crops is that they are grown to prepare the soil in preparation for growing other crops. They are known as green-manure crops, with the specific purpose of building and maintaining soil fertility and soil structure. Grown during the same season of the year as vegetable crops, they are turned under while they are still green and are usually put back into the soil, either directly, or afterwards, once they have been removed and composted.

Cover crops are grown with a dual purpose, both soil protection and soil improvement, and are only grown throughout the seasons when vegetable crops are not grown. By turning over a soil-improving crop and returning it to the soil the nutrients which contributed to the growth of the crop add to the quantity of organic matter. Legumes, plants such as bean and peas which form fruits and seeds in pods, and non-legumes, are effective soil-improving crops, but legumes are more valuable as they contribute nitrogen and humus. How quickly plant materials decompose depends on the type of crop, its stage of growth, the soil temperature and levels of moisture. The greater the moisture in the material when it's turned over, the more rapidly it decomposes, as opposed to drier materials which breakdown more slowly. If you are turning over drier materials it is better to turn under soil-improving crops before they reach maturity, unless enough time has passed between ploughing and the planting of your next set of crops. In order to decompose quickly, plant materials need warmth and moisture. If the soil is dry, little or no decomposition will occur until rain or irrigation creates the required moisture.

A small field can yield a plentiful supply of crops.

Crop rotation is the sequence of growing different types of crops on the same plot throughout the growing seasons. Rotating crops around your plot reduces the dependence on a single group of nutrients, not to mention the reducing the likelihood of cultivating resistant pest and weeds. It is important because it helps control disease and insects whilst encouraging better use of the soil resources.

A practice of clean culture is often followed in vegetable growing. The soil is managed by not over cultivating, keeping it free of all competing plants, and through regular cultivation, protective coverings, weed killers and mulches. This clean vegetable field management practice reduces the probability of attacks by insects and disease-incitant organisms.

Plot location

Take your time to assess the situation of your plot. Is it sheltered or exposed to weather conditions? Is it on a slope? What direction does the plot face? Where is the sunrise and where is the sunset? How much sunlight does the plot enjoy in the summer, and in the winter? These are key questions that will affect the growing conditions of your plants.

The perfect location is an open site, which enjoys sunshine throughout the daylight hours but is protected from strong winds. The site would ideally be supported with access to a good water supply.

Soil and sunlight are key elements to perfect growing conditions.

Climate and soil

From a growing perspective the combination of soil and climate are the most important elements when creating the perfect growing conditions for your plants. Plants require rich, fertile soil and lots of water, warmth and sunshine. Your first job is to work out the soil type at your plot. Is it sticky, heavy, water retentive clay, or light, sandy soil that drains easily? Is it acid, alkaline or neutral? Acid soils are low in calcium and can need lime or lime-rich composts to make them more alkaline. Alkaline soils can be more difficult but again certain composts can be added such as sawdust or pine bark to make them more acidic. The best course of action is to buy a pH test kit which will reveal the pH levels of your soil.

The weather where you live is a given over which you have little control. The best course of action is to tailor your growing to fruit and vegetables which are best suited to the conditions that nature's hand has dealt you.

The most important factors are temperature and rainfall. Temperature is responsible for the plant processes, including: germination, growth of roots, photosynthesis and also how well nutrients are absorbed from the soil. Water is necessary for plants to grow.

Beginner's tool kit

As with any new hobby it's easy to overspend when buying gardening tools. They can take up a lot space and cost a lot of money, but staying focused on the basics can keep your shed or storage area from becoming overcrowded. There's always bigger and better, but buying the best quality tools that your budget will allow, and maintaining them, can go a long way in getting the most out of your investment. When you are more seasoned you can work out which tools work best for you. There are no hard and fast rules.

FROM POT TO PATCH

The right tools lighten the load.

Here are 12 essential garden tools:

1. Gloves

While gardening can be a wonderful hobby, it can quickly turn into a thorny and splintery hassle without the right pair of gloves.

- Gloves should be durable but not too bulky, especially for working with seeds or transplanting seedlings.
- Fit is important, as poorly fitting gloves can cause blisters or result in accidents from slipping off.
- Fabrics that are water resistant but also breathable will help keep hands cool and comfortable.
- Longer cuffs protect wrists and forearms from scratches and keep soil from getting in.
- Store gloves out of sunlight, away from water and safe from insects.

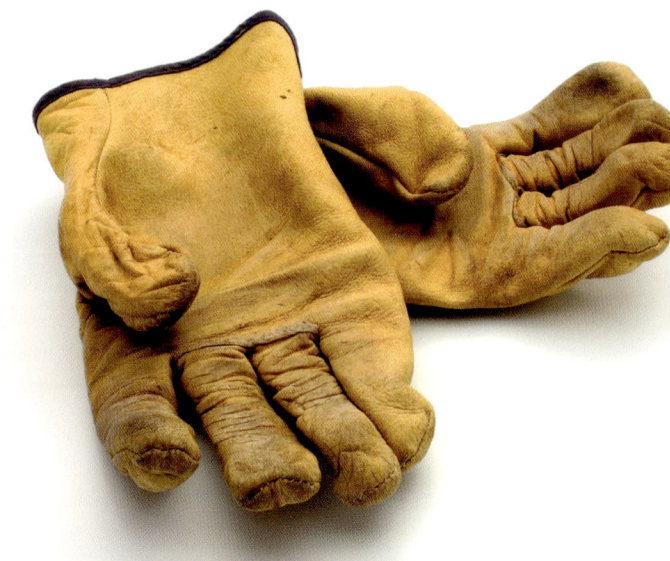

GROW YOUR OWN FOOD

A simple selection of the right tools is all you need.

2. Garden fork

An efficient tool for turning soil, a garden fork can dig into dense soil better than a spade.

- Forks with a slight curve to the spines are useful for scooping mulch or turning compost piles, much like a pitchfork.
- Straight tines are better for digging, and great for compacted, rocky, or clay soil.
- Square tines are stronger than flat tines, which can bend when they hit a rock or root.

3. Hand trowel

The essential hand tool, trowels are wonderful for hand digging bedding plants and herbs, planting containers, and taking out weeds.

- Select a broad blade to move more soil or a long, narrow blade to dig up weeds or for rocky soil.
- The handle should fit comfortably in your hand.
- Trowels forged from stainless steel, or at least with a stainless steel head, are more durable and will last longer.

FROM POT TO PATCH

4. Pruning shears

Hand pruners, also called secateurs, help trim plants that are getting out of control and taking over. Anvil-style pruners cut with a sharp blade meeting a flat surface, similar to a knife on a board. Bypass pruners cut with a sharp blade passing by a sharp-edged flat surface, more like scissors.

- Anvil pruners are good for dead wood but can cause crush injuries to fresh, green stems and branches.
- Bypass pruners are useful for live plants and green wood.
- Pruners should fit easily in the palm of your hand.
- Ratcheting pruners provide increased cutting strength, perfect for anyone with reduced hand strength or arthritis.
- For cleaner cuts and less injury to plants, pruners should be sharpened regularly.

5. Spade

These short-handled square shovels are garden workhorses. They make easy work of digging holes for plants, edging, lifting sod, and moving small mounds of dirt from one area to another. A good spade will last you the rest of your gardening life so is worth investing in.

- Treads on top of the blade give a sturdier and more comfortable foot surface when needing an extra push.
- Ash hardwood handles are durable, and absorb shock and vibration.
- Spades are available with long or short handles. Longer handles provide more leverage, but are heavier.
- Stainless steel heads are strong and won't rust.

6. Rake

A sturdy rake is essential for garden clearing. Rakes come in a wide variety of styles and sizes, but a great starter is a standard leaf rake.
- Adjustable rakes do the job of more than one tool, reaching into narrow areas or gathering large piles of leaves.
- Steel tines are stronger although may be rougher on delicate lawns than plastic tines.

7. Hoe

For a veggie garden you will need a sturdy, wide hoe. Hoes are useful in preparing garden and flower beds and cutting down weeds.
- Look for a comfortable handle with a long reach.
- A sharp blade works better and is easier to use.
- Weeding hoes, also called hula or stirrup hoes, have an open square head and are pushed back and forth just under the soil surface to cut down top growth.
- Flat hoes are good for turning the soil in rows in vegetable gardens.

FROM POT TO PATCH

8. Loppers

Another cutting tool, loppers are basically long-handled pruners used to trim hard-to-reach areas and cut thicker branches. The long handles provide the leverage it takes to cut through branches up to 25mm or more in diameter. There are anvil and bypass types, just like pruners. Handles generally range from 40 to 91cm.

- Bypass loppers are more precise in cut location than anvil style.
- Like pruners, keep lopper blades in good condition and sharpen regularly.
- Longer handled loppers can be heavy. Know what you'll be cutting and how far you'll need to reach, and get the appropriate length.
- Lightweight aluminium or carbon-composite handles can be lighter.

9. Garden hose with adjustable nozzle

Water is key and it's important that your garden hose can reach and spray every area. There are three basic hose diameters: 1.2cm (avg 41 litres per minute), 1.2–2.0cm (avg 68.2 litres per minute), and 2cm (up to 112 litres per minute). An adjustable nozzle puts you in control of the water pressure and spray radius.

- Estimate the amount of length you will need with your hose before buying one.
- Hose length will affect water pressure – the longer the hose, the lower the resulting pressure.
- Vinyl hoses are lighter weight and less expensive, but kink easier and don't last as long as rubber construction.
- Store hoses coiled up and out of direct sunlight. Storing with kinks in them can result in weak spots.

GROW YOUR OWN FOOD

10. Watering wand

Give your plants a gentle rain shower with a water-breaking wand. The extended reach is also helpful to get to out-of-the-way containers, hanging plants, or the back edges of borders. Watering wands come in a variety of lengths, from 25 to 120cm.

- Choose an appropriate length for your needs – longer for high hanging baskets, shorter for tighter spaces.
- Built-in shut off valves in the handle conserve water and allow you to adjust the flow.

11. Watering can

There are two basic types of watering can, plastic or metal. There are hundreds of styles, colours, sizes and nozzle options.

- Plastic cans can be lighter than metal, but won't last as long.
- Metal cans should be galvanised to resist rusting.
- Consider the size of the can relative to your strength; 4.5 litres (1 gallon) of water weighs just over 3.6kg.
- The handle position should allow you to carry a full can and also tip it to pour easily.
- Two-handled designs allow for better stability for children or elderly gardeners.
- You may need two: a larger one with a sprinkler head for outdoors, and a smaller, long-necked version for houseplants.

A wheelbarrow is handy for moving heavy loads.

12. Wheelbarrow

If your garden has extra soil to be moved around, compost or mulch that needs to be added to garden beds, or any other heavy lifting and moving project, a wheelbarrow can help you move large volumes of material.

- Traditional dual-handle, single wheel styles can be harder to balance with heavy or unevenly distributed loads.
- Single-handle two-wheel models are easier to balance, better for those with limited strength or when pulling over uneven terrain.
- Single-handled wheelbarrows can be pushed or pulled with one hand.
- Store it clean and dry to prevent rust.
- Keep the wheels properly inflated for easier wheeling.

 GROW YOUR OWN FOOD

CHAPTER 2

The Seed of an Idea

A key step in your food growing journey is deciding which seeds to choose. The seed is the origin of the process and the choice is wide and varied. But it can feel complex. On reading the seed packets there are descriptions such as: hybrid, open-pollinated, organic, conventional, naturally grown, and heirloom. But what do they mean? And how do they influence your decision?

The seed is the origin of the plant.

THE SEED OF AN IDEA 25

Choosing seeds is a very personal decision.

Garden seeds - two key types

The two key types of seeds are decided by how they were grown or bred: either open-pollinated or hybrid.

Open-pollinated
The seeds are created as a result of pollination from insects, birds or wind.

Are open-pollinated seeds for you?
Open-pollinated seeds can produce plants that are identical to the parent plant, known as 'true-to-type', and are also called heirloom seeds. If you have a much-loved flavour from your plant which you want to continue growing then this a reliable way of ensuring a continuation of your favourite flavours. It is worth noting that not all open-pollinated seeds are heirlooms; however, all heirloom seeds are classified as open-pollinated. These seeds are enjoyed and passed down from generation to generation of food growers.

What happens if an insect accidentally cross-pollinates a cucumber and a melon? The seeds are open-pollinated because it occurred naturally, but they're also a hybrid. Some open-pollinated seeds are 'true-to-type' and others are hybrids. This a frequent occurrence in small gardens and provides a plethora of strange and delicious seed variations. While these open-pollinated anomalies are technically hybrids, a seed packet labelled as a hybrid means that it was intentionally created. Cucamelons are a great example. Often described as tasting like a

GROW YOUR OWN FOOD

High yield hybrids increase your odds of a successful garden.

cucumber crossed with a lime, they are the size of a grape, with the pattern of a watermelon... no wonder people think they're engineered! In actual fact they're just a wild form of cucumber that grows naturally in Mexico (an incredibly biodiverse country with hundreds of thousands of native plants).

These plants haven't been genetically modified. They're just F1 generation crosses from two different parents. This style of seed has what's known as 'hybrid vigour' which boosts growth. It is also hard or impossible to save seeds from F1s. And any you do save won't be the same as their parent. So that's why seed companies love selling them – because we can't save our own seed from them!

Hybrids

Hybrid seeds refers to the intentional cross pollination of two plants to create desired qualities – such as flavour, yield, resistance to disease or heat tolerance. The creation of hybrids has been happening for centuries to make it easier to grow food that is predictable, tastier, abundant and more aptly suited for travel or storage. Cross pollination can simply be achieved by using a paintbrush to transfer the pollen from one plant to another.

Why select hybrid seeds for your garden?
Learning how to grow your own food can be a journey of trial and error. If you're embarking on growing food for the first time, it might be worth choosing high-yield hybrids to increase your chances of a successful garden.

THE SEED OF AN IDEA

Can you use the hybrid seeds from your homegrown plants?
As mentioned earlier, if you save the seeds from your planted hybrid plants, the next generation may or may not have the same traits as the original seeds. However, if you don't mind surprises it can be fun to see what happens, if a little unpredictable.

If you planted a hybrid tomato plant, took two seeds from it, and planted them, one of these seeds could grow into a plant that produces few fruit – but with a similar flavour to the original – while the other could provide a plentiful supply of delicious fruit yet with completely different appearance and flavour. It is possible to save hybrid seeds… but prepare to be surprised!

What is the difference between organic, conventional and naturally grown seeds?

These terms are often found on a seed packet but what do they mean? Naturally grown may sound good but it means nothing. It simply describes seeds that are not certified organic. It is worth buying organic, because chemical residue is systemic and can impact on pollinators.

What does organic mean?
Organic seeds are harvested from certified organic plants, meaning the parent plant has fulfilled the organic requirements. Some small-scale farmers grow seeds organically, but don't pay for the expensive organic certification. Usually, a seed company will inform you if the seeds are grown organically but are uncertified. However, in some cases you might have to take the grower's word for it. If you want more provenance then ask the seed supplier and explore the marketplace to find suppliers that you can trust.

So why not just buy the cheaper conventional seed and grow it organically? Does this make your food organic?

There's some debate about the quantity of toxins which remain in seeds of a plant which is grown conventionally. Whilst what happens after planting is what matters, some toxins could persist. If a home gardener wants a totally clean product it is more reliable to buy organic seeds to ensure integrity.

Seed selection

On the whole, most home gardeners select a mixture of open-pollinated, hybrid, and heirloom seeds. It is a case of trial and error and discovering your taste, preference, and values, which could change from season to season.

Understanding the labels on your seed packets means you can make informed decisions and embark on a growing journey. There is no right or wrong answer but instead exploration and learning, which should be fun along the way.

Choose seeds to your taste and lifestyle

Choose varieties of fruits and vegetables which suit your needs. Each variety comes in many different sizes and types. You may focus on flavour, a specific size, high yields, fast growth, or other priorities.

It makes sense to grow things that you and your family like but it can also be fun to experiment and try new things. When selecting your garden seeds, be sure your mix up your selection. It's best to grow a variety of crops. Biodiversity prevents pests and soil degradation but also gives a diverse harvest that provides more nutrients for you and your family.

Plan your seed planting and priorities.

CHAPTER 3

Propagation

The purpose of propagation is to produce seedlings by germinating seeds, growing cuttings or by using methods to support plant reproduction and growth. Propagation takes different forms dependent on the type of plants you want to grow. The amount of time required can vary depending on the method. Plants are propagated in various rooting mediums.

Potting choices are plentiful.

Rooting mediums

The variations on the medium used for rooting cuttings is dependent on either the species and the materials to hand.

These are the most common rooting mediums:

Water: This is good for easily rooting species. However, the lack of aeration is a disadvantage. Artificial aeration in the water encourages rooting and slows down the rotting process.

Sand: Any sand needs to be fine enough to hold some moisture around the cutting and yet coarse enough to drain freely. The sand needs to be washed and sterilised prior to use. It is worth noting that beach sand is highly concentrated in salt and this could be toxic to some plants.

Soil: Using a well aerated sandy loam – a fertile soil of clay and sand containing humus – is preferable. If you are using soil that has been previously used there may be the presence of root-borne disease so it may need sterilising before use.

Peat moss: Used in-conjunction with other materials to increase the water holding capacity.

Vegetable Propagation

Propagation of vegetables, involving the creation and development of new individual plants in the establishment of new plantings, is achieved by the use of seeds or the vegetative parts of plants.

Using seeds is known as sexual propagation, and is used for plants such as: asparagus, bean, broccoli, cabbage, carrot, cauliflower, celery, cucumber, eggplant, leek, lettuce, onion, parsley, pea, pepper, pumpkin, radish, spinach, sweet corn squash, tomato, and turnip.

Using the vegetative part of the plant is called asexual propagation, and is used for plants such as: artichokes, garlic, potatoes, rhubarb, and sweet potato.

Asexual propagation

Vegetable propagation involves producing new plants using vegetative parts of the plants, such as roots, leaves and stems. As the new plant grows from the parent plant there is no genetic exchange, so that plants grown are identical to the parent plant and are also known as clones.

This process of propagation by cuttings can be by either division, layering, grafting and budding. Taking cuttings isn't complicated and is a cheap method of creating new plants from an existing one, but often requires a splash of patience to get them to root.

Two common methods of taking cuttings are softwood and hardwood cuttings.

Cuttings require patience.

Cuttings

Softwood are cuttings from young shoots early in the year, unlike hardwood cuttings, which are cut from woody shoots at the end of each growing season. Softwood cuttings are needier than hardwood cuttings but are usually quicker to root and begin growing. It's relatively easy to root new plants from cuttings, but taking a bit of extra care can help ensure success. Patience is required, however, because the time it takes to create new roots can be around three to four weeks, depending on the type of plant. Hardwood cuttings can take even longer, up to a year to develop decent roots, but they need very little care other than the occasional watering.

Cutting toolkit
Sharp knife or scissors
Bags to collect cuttings
Multi-purpose potting compost
Grit
Labels
Hormone rooting powder

For softwood cuttings:
Dibber or pencil
Small pots (around 9cm)
Covered propagator, or clear bags, to cover cuttings
Multi-purpose compost with 30% sand added

PROPAGATION

Cut away
Take softwood cuttings during mid-spring to early summer and hardwood cuttings from mid-autumn to mid-winter.

Softwood cuttings tips
First, fill your pots with compost and water them so that they are ready for the cuttings.

It's best to snip the cuttings early in the day as the plants' stems are full of water. Use a bag to stop them drying out and pop them in the pot as soon as you can.

When taking a cutting, select a strong shoot and cut a piece between 5–10cm long.

Remove all leaves from the lower half of the cutting and pinch off the growing tip.

Dab the end of the cutting in hormone rooting powder to aid the cutting in the production of roots, which reduces the risk of bacterial infection.

Make a hole in the centre of a pot filled with compost, using the dibber or pencil, and insert the cutting, making sure there is some of the cutting above the surface. Press the compost down around the cutting.

After potting up all the cuttings, label the pots and either place in a propagator with a lid, or cover each pot with a clear plastic bag, and keep them in a place with bright, but indirect light. Ventilation is important so open the propagator vents daily, or remove the plastic bags for 10 minutes regularly.

Choose a hardy woody shoot.

GROW YOUR OWN FOOD

Water often to keep the compost moist. Cuttings can take between 6 and 10 weeks to root. Keep an eye on the pots' drainage holes for signs of the roots appearing.

Once the cuttings have taken, place the pots outside during the day and bring them in at night for about two weeks to make them hardier.

Following this, re-plant them into larger pots until they are big enough to plant out if necessary.

Hardwood cuttings tips

Autumn is the best time to take hardwood cuttings after the plants have dropped their leaves and are dormant. Avoid taking cuttings in frosty weather.

If you want to take several cuttings, ready a narrow trench in a sheltered spot outside. The cuttings will grow for most of the following year in the trench. Drainage is key, so add a layer of sand to the base of the trench, and then load it up with soil mixed with compost. If you are only taking a few cuttings you can use pots filled with a 50/50 mix of multipurpose compost and grit.

Select a hardy, pencil-thick woody shoot which has grown in the current year and cut it off close to the base of the shoot. Cut off the tip of the shoot and section it into lengths 15–30cm long. Slice it above a bud at the top of each length, with a sloping cut. This removes rainfall from the cutting and indicates which end of the cutting is which.

Below a bud at the bottom of each cutting, make a straight cut.

Fill a pot with hormone rooting powder and dip the lower end of each cutting in.

Plant the lower ends of the cuttings into the soil where they will be housed. Make sure that one-third of each cutting is above the soil. Keep the cuttings around 15cm apart if planting in trenches.

Keep the cuttings in the same place until the next autumn. Water when necessary to ensure the compost doesn't dry out. Finally, when the cuttings have taken root, they can be replanted in their permanent home.

What are the best plants to take cuttings from?

Once you know how to take a cutting from a plant, there are plenty of suitable plants to choose from. Softwood cuttings are ideal for many deciduous shrubs, including lavender and rosemary. Hardwood cuttings work well for most deciduous shrubs, as well as climbers like grape vines, and fruit bushes such as blackcurrants, redcurrants, gooseberries and figs.

Taking cuttings allows plants that do not produce seeds to be grown using a single parent plant, so do not require pollination or cross-pollination. Asexual propagation is quicker than sexual propagation and the plant can inherit beneficial traits from the parent plant.

Other forms of asexual propagation:

Leaf cutting

This is like stem cuttings, apart from cutting a leaf stalk and not the main stem. There are a few different ways of leaf cuttings and the method you use will depend on the type of plant you are cutting from. Removing the leaf and stalk from the parent plant and then placing it directly upright into the rooting medium works for some plants. For others, some of the small veins on the leaf need to be slit, with the leaf placed horizontally over the rooting medium.

Rooted stems can create new plants.

Division

Some plants grow with several stems having roots attached to each stem. The rooted stems can be parted from the parent plant to create a new plant. As long as the stems are not joined they can be gently separated, or they will need to be divided using a sharp knife. Once they have been divided they can be individually potted in the rooting medium to grow.

Layering

This enables a stem to create its own roots whilst still attached to the parent plant. There are many types of layering including tip, simple, compound, mound and air layering. In principle though they each follow a similar method.

This is where a stem, or multiple parts of a stem, from the parent plant are blended to come into contact with or are placed in a rooting medium. A slit is cut into the underside of the piece of stem that is in the rooting medium, which enables new roots to form, which can then be separated from the parent plant and potted.

Grafting and budding

This is where plant sections are joined together to grow as a single plant because they do not root well as cuttings, or their own root systems are not up to the job. To graft a plant the upper part of one plant grows on the root system of another plant. However, with budding, a bud is cut from one plant and then grown on another. Don't dismay if this is beyond your talents, as it is considered the trickiest of propagation methods; therefore it is mainly practised by experienced nurseries and gardeners.

Sexual propagation

Both male and female plants contribute to create a new plant in a natural process. This where a parent species forms an offspring with different genetics to the parent plants. The process starts with flowering, and then pollination, fertilisation and in the end seed formation. The newly created seeds form completely new plants when sown. This method of propagation is simple, easy and economical.

Sexual propagation is essential for some plant, tree, vegetable or fruit species as it is the only way they can reproduce. The outcome is the creation of a new, better, crop species that is more robust and disease-resistant with a longer life span, whilst at the same time also preventing viral transmission from parent plants.

This is the only process which enables large numbers of crops to be planted, all with genetic variation. The method is responsible for the continuous evolution of plants and ensures the improved production of better offspring. The created seeds are easy to transport and store.

Vegetable and fruit types

The classification of vegetables is according to the part of the plant which is eaten. Some vegetables exist in multiple categories, as multiple parts of the plant can be eaten; for example, both the roots and leaves of beetroot are edible.

Onions are rich in nutrients.

Carrots are root vegetable crops.

Bulbs

Onions, garlic, leeks.

As part of the Allium species, bulb vegetables store the nutrients in the bulb of the vegetable and tend to grow underground. The nutrients provided by these vegetables are significant and they are considered to be essential to support healthy skin, eyes, and the functioning of the central nervous system. The most popular bulb vegetables are onion, chive, spring onion and garlic. These bulb vegetables are considered to be medicinal, especially onion and garlic.

Root and tubers

Carrot, radish, turnip, beets, potato, sweet potato.

Root vegetables and tubers are geophytes, grown under the soil and brim with nutrients gained from the soil. Whilst all tubers are root vegetables, not all root vegetables are tubers. They are appropriately named because the heart of the crop is the downward growing root of the plant. Above ground grows the green elements, and beneath the ground grows the root.

Tubers are slightly different as they form at the base of the root and store energy while supporting new stem growth. Like root vegetables the green elements are above the ground, but instead below ground there is a system of roots from which the tubers grow. It's possible to grow several tubers from a single above ground plant, whereas root crops have a single root vegetable from each plant.

To confuse matters, some bulb vegetables, such as garlic and ginger, and also some stem vegetables are sometimes categorised as root vegetables. Root vegetables are low in fats and are a fantastic source of proteins and carbohydrates.

Stem vegetables have edible roots and stalks.

Stem

Asparagus, kohlrabi, rhubarb, celery.

Stem vegetables have shoots or stalks which can be eaten. These vegetables are loaded with minerals, vitamins and antioxidants.

Leaf vegetables are edible leaves.

Fruits carry the seeds of the plants.

Leaf

Cabbage, kale, lettuce, spinach.

Leaf vegetables are the edible leaves of the vegetable. They are rich in potassium, iron, magnesium, calcium, folic acid and certain phyto-chemicals. Eating green leafy vegetables every day reduces the risk of diseases such as high blood pressure, diabetes, cancer and heart diseases.

Fruits

Aubergine, capsicum, tomato, pumpkin, cucumber.

Fruit vegetables are defined botanically because they meet the definition of fruits. Scientifically, they are deemed to be fruits because they carry the seeds of the plants.

Flowering vegetables are named due to their flower shape.

Seed vegetables are rich in protein.

Flower
Cauliflower, broccoli, artichokes.

Flowering vegetables are named because they are flower shaped. They contain phyto-chemicals called as 'isothiocyanates' which can help prevent the production of cancerous cells.

Seeds
Pea, soybeans, French bean.

Known also as podded vegetables, seed vegetables are a rich source of proteins and also contain potassium, folic acid, complex carbohydrates, magnesium, iron, fibre and zinc.

Types of fruit

Simple fruits grow from a single ovary.

Simple fruits
A simple fruit is one that develops from a single ovary in a single flower. Simple fruits can be fleshy or dry. There are three types of fleshy simple fruit: the berry, the drupe, and the pome.

Berry
Cranberries, blueberries, redcurrants, bananas, tomatoes, peppers and cucumbers.

To confuse us all any small fleshy fruit is often called a berry, more so if it is edible. Yet Raspberries, blackberries and strawberries are not actually berries but instead are classified as aggregate fruits. Cranberries and blueberries, however, are true botanical berries but so are fruits that have many seeds, such as bananas.

Drupe
Peaches, coconut, olives.

This is a fleshy fruit with single seed and a hard endocarp.

Pome
Pears, apples.

The fruit is grown from the receptacle (under the flower).

Hesperirdium
Orange, lemon, grapefruit.

These fruits are covered in a leathery rind with a tough and fibrous carpel.

Aggregate fruit
Strawberries, blackberries, raspberries.

These are fruits that consist of a number of smaller fruits developed from one flower with many pistils.

Dry simple fruits are categorised as either dehiscent or indehiscent. Dry dehiscent fruits crack open along two seams and shed their seeds into the environment when the fruit is ripe.

Legumes are the edible seeds of a plant.

Legumes
Beans, peas, peanuts.

A legume is the edible seed of a plant which grows from a flower and into a pod. The pod has a seam which runs down the side. Botanically, they are fruits but are often classified as vegetables.

Capsules
Brazil nut, horse chestnut.

Capsules are simple, dry though rarely fleshy, splitting fruit. The capsule releases its seeds and splits apart.

Nuts
Hazelnuts, almonds, pecan.

Nuts have one seed and a hard pericarp. Nuts do not release seeds as they are a compound ovary containing both a single seed and the fruit.

Grains
Wheat, rice, barley.

Grains are the dry fruits of grasses and are harvested when they are on the plant. They are not seeds, but they do house the seeds of grasses. This defines the grains as fruits as they are the seed bearing section of a flowering plant.

Multiple fruits
Pineapples, figs, mulberries.

Multiple fruits are bunches of simple fruits, which have grown together to form the multiple fruits. The fruits have come from several different flowers and have joined together.

Garden planning helps you keep on top of the tasks.

When to sow the seed

January

January	Plant
In the UK January is a cold month so it's often a quiet month in the garden. However, if your green fingers are twitching then it is a good time to sow seeds in your greenhouse, windowsill, heated propagator or under cover. It's important that you can keep the seeds warm and moist because a cold seed won't grow. January is a good time to sow broad beans in pots, if the weather is mild, and then placing them in a cold frame or unheated greenhouse. In the greenhouse, sow aubergines, summer cabbages and cauliflower. You can also sow some early crops of lettuces, spinach, spring onions and turnips. In a heated propagator sow onion seeds. **January jobs** It's a good time to clear up dropped leaves and clear greenhouse gutters. Clean the greenhouse glass. Empty and clean out water-butts. Prep and organise your trays and pots. Clean your tools and equipment, and service any machinery, such as your lawn mower. Dig over empty ground, forking in plenty of rotted manure or compost. Use polythene sheets to prevent waterlogging and then once the soil has dried out carry on digging out. Raise any planted pots from the ground and put them in a sheltered position.	Broad beans Aubergines Leeks Cress Carrots Onions Lemon grass Shallots Lettuce Tomato Cauliflower Kale Strawberry Pea shoots

PROPAGATION

January — Plant

January is cold and quiet.

Vegetables

Store seed potatoes in trays, in a light, cool, frost-free place to encourage sprouting, ready for planting in March or April. Sow broad beans if conditions are suitable and not too cold. In the greenhouse you could also sow aubergine and summer cauliflower.

If you live in a colder area sow onions in your greenhouse, then harden off the plants in March so they are ready to be planted outdoors in April.

For summer grown runner beans, prepare a deep trench, situated where you are planning to grow them, by digging out and filling with compost. In late spring cover with soil and sow the beans on top.

Fruit

If the soil conditions are suitable plant raspberries and other soft cane fruit. However, if it's too cold then plant them temporarily elsewhere or pot them to stop the roots drying out. Prune established fruit bushes and trees.

Whitecurrants and redcurrants need old stems removed to avoid over-crowding in the middle. Prune the side shoots back to a single bud.

Protect dormant clumps of early rhubarb with buckets or jars placed over them to encourage stems to develop, giving an early harvest.

Any potted nectarine and peach trees should be moved under cover for the winter to protect them and the early flowers. Rain damage can cause the spread of peach leaf curl disease.

FEBRUARY

February	Plant
Despite the evenings slowly getting lighter and the sense that spring is teasingly close, February is still cold. Outside you can sow early carrots, parsnips and broad beans. In your greenhouse, or heated propagator, you can plant the seeds of chillies, cabbage, celery, parsley, peppers, tomato, leek and onions. You can also plant shallot sets, from mid February onwards. Varieties of potatoes which are ready early can be chitted (sprouts shooting from the potato) in preparation for planting towards the end of March. February is also a good time to order asparagus crowns and to begin prepping the asparagus beds.	Brussels sprouts Carrot Cabbage Cress Cauliflower Sweet basil Parsnip Cucumber Parsley

February is a good time to prepare.

PROPAGATION

February

February jobs

Weather wise, February is unpredictable but it can still be a busy time of the year for gardeners as preparation is king.

To prevent your soil becoming waterlogged, especially if it is heavy clay, protect it with polythene secured by bricks or planks of wood. As a temporary fixture it is easy to fold it back and dig over the soil and then re-install it.

Another method is to cover the soil with compost or manure, and then lightly fork the surface which prepares the soil for planting. If you are planning to early sow then it is worth warming the soil up by a few degrees. A few weeks beforehand cover the soil by using a single layer of polythene or fleece. This method encourages germination.

Cold frames can provide additional winter protection for plants. Make sure they are placed in full sunlight and protected from the cold February winds. Ventilation is key so it's worth opening up on warm days to prevent overheating but it is also important to remember to close again at night when the temperature drops. If it's really cold at night then a rug over the frame will help protect the plants within.

Vegetables

Chit potatoes (lay out in trays so they sprout) in a cool, light, frost-free place, which increases the yield of the tubers. This is in preparation for planting near the end of March.

In your greenhouse or warm propagator, seeds such as cabbage (summer/autumn maturing), celery, parsley, sweet and cayenne pepper, tomato, leek and onion can be planted.

Under your outdoor cold frame early varieties of carrot, broad bean and parsnip can be sown. Mid month you can plant out shallots.

Asparagus crowns should be ordered in good time for a late March/early April delivery. It's a good time to start prepping your patch of ground to put them in.

Fruit

February is a good time to prune established fruit trees and bushes before any growth commences, so crops can prosper. On trained gooseberry bushes prune side shoots back to two or three buds. Cover rhubarb crowns with buckets to encourage early pickings, separate and lift any congested clumps.

Outdoor grapevines need to be pruned, shortening the fruited shoots and therefore encouraging new growth.

Prune large apple and pear trees and remove any branches getting in the way.

Plant soft fruit if the weather permits.

Plant

Mint
Broad beans
Tomatoes
Chilli peppers
Leaf salad
Salad onions
Leeks
Peas
Sweet peppers
Beetroot
Lettuce
Aubergine
Spinach
Asparagus
Tarragon
Sage
Broccoli
Bean sprouts
Shallots
Strawberries
Artichoke
Kale
Radish
Lemongrass
Mustard
Squash
Onions

MARCH

March	Plant
With March comes warmer temperatures. The soil is warming up and it's a great time to sow vegetables. Sow artichoke, beetroot, parsley, spinach, aubergine, cucumber, early varieties of tomatoes, fruit and tender veggies in a heated greenhouse or a heated propagator. These will develop well on plants when grown under glass in a heated greenhouse. For outdoor varieties sow later in the month, so as they grow they can be planted out in early June.	Carrot
	Cabbage
	Cress
	Cauliflower
	Sweet basil
	Parsnip
	Cucumber
Vegetables	Parsley
Early sowings can be made if the ground isn't too wet by making sure the soil is warmed up beforehand with polythene or fleece which will help to ensure good seed germination results. Once the soil conditions are suitable sow artichoke, beetroot, broad bean, Brussels sprouts, cabbage, cauliflower, carrot, lettuce, parsley, spinach, aubergine and cucumber, along with other tender vegetables, in a heated greenhouse.	Mint
	Broad beans
	Tomatoes
	Chilli peppers
	Leaf salad

March shoots towards spring.

PROPAGATION

March

Space shallot sets at 15cm intervals in rows 30cm apart, and once conditions have warmed up towards the end of March, onion sets can be planted.

Sow parsley in pots for a plentiful summer and divide chives into clumps and pot them.

Early varieties of tomatoes will prosper when grown under glass in a heated greenhouse. To speed up germination, sow the seed in a heated propagator or in covered trays on a sunny windowsill. Later in the month sow outdoor varieties and pot the plants as they grow, ready for planting outside in early June.

March is also a good month to chit potatoes in trays so that the shoots form. It's ok to plant early varieties of potatoes during March, but for the main crop varieties it's better to plant in April.

During March and April celery seed can be sown into pots then placed in the greenhouse so you will have plants ready for planting out during May and June.

Fruit

Having pruned established trees and bushes previously these should be left to thrive; however, you can still make late plantings of soft fruit such as gooseberry, raspberry and strawberry.

To encourage long, tender stalks of rhubarb cover the crowns with old buckets or tubs to keep out the light.

Raised beds and cold frames

If you have raised beds March is a good time to get them ready for early seed sowings from mid-April onwards.

Warm the soil in the beds by covering them with black sheeting. The black absorbs the sunlight. The sheeting also draws out slugs which can be easily removed.

Portable polythene tunnels serve to trap heat in the soil and also protect the young seedlings. Crops such as beetroot, carrots, parsnip, radish and spring onions are all suitable to be grown in them.

Plant

- Salad onions
- Leeks
- Peas
- Sweet peppers
- Beetroot
- Lettuce
- Aubergine
- Spinach
- Asparagus
- Tarragon
- Sage
- Broccoli
- Bean sprouts
- Shallots
- Mint
- Brussels sprouts
- Strawberries
- Artichoke
- Kale
- Radish
- Lemongrass
- Mustard
- Squash
- Onions
- Sweetcorn
- Courgette
- Dwarf beans
- Chives
- Pak choi
- Peppers
- Celeriac
- Oregano
- Broad beans
- Melon
- Rhubarb
- Pumpkin
- Cornichons
- Dill
- Runner beans
- Endives
- Turnip

GROW YOUR OWN FOOD

April

April	Plant
Spring is springing, the weather is beginning to warm up, although frosts can still occur, so don't be lulled into a false sense of security. If a frost is forecast, protect your potatoes with some cover. April is the time to sow carrots, peas, beetroot, winter cabbages, broccoli, salad crops and more. In a heated greenhouse or propagator, you can sow marrows, courgettes, pumpkins, squashes and tomatoes. **Vegetables** April is the time to sow seeds of your choice such as carrots, peas, beetroot, winter cabbages, broccoli, salad crops and more. Sow marrows, courgettes, pumpkins, squashes and tomatoes in a heated greenhouse or propagator. If a frost threatens cover the plants with horticultural fleece, straw or anything light which won't crush the plants but will cover them and protect them from the frost. The second option is to do an early earthing up. Only do it for frost damage limitation purposes and cover the potato plants entirely with soil.	Carrot Cabbage Cress Cauliflower Sweet basil Parsnip Cucumber Parsley Mint Broad beans Tomatoes Chilli peppers Leaf salad Salad onions Leeks Peas Marrow

By April spring is springing.

PROPAGATION

April

Plant onion sets when the soil is dry.

If you already have a clump of rhubarb in your garden cut back any flowers that appear. Cut them out near the base as they will steal food and energy from the plant.

If you have established asparagus beds of at least two years old then cut any spears using a sharp knife, or treat yourself to a made-for-purpose asparagus knife.

Fruit

Mulch improves the soil around trees so cover the roots of your fruit trees with a well-rotted manure.

Apple trees, pear trees, plum trees and cherry trees will blossom in April. If as little as 5 to 10% of the flowers set then you will have a good crop, so don't worry too much about flowers dropping.

Stake newly planted trees to prevent wind rock and movement of the roots. This can tear new roots, which slows down establishment of the tree. A newly planted tree can take a few of years to anchor itself in the soil.

If it's a dry month then regularly water all newly planted trees.

If you have established summer and autumn fruiting raspberry canes they should be cut back to approximately 23cm from the base.

Garden cloches are low enclosures used to cover plants and they can provide protection. They can shield against harsh weather, pest attack and provide a warm microclimate to encourage germinating seedlings, young plants and crops. To encourage early flowers in your strawberry plants, cover the plants with cloches.

Herbs

Fresh herbs are wonderful additions to your life and don't require lots of space. Sow dill, fennel, hyssop, parsley, coriander, basil and thyme.

Any sowings made in March may need careful thinning, which means separating the seedlings so they can become single plants.

If you have an established thyme plant try layering some of the creeping stems by covering them with fine soil. Rooted plants can be separated and planted elsewhere.

Plant

Sweet peppers
Beetroot
Lettuce
Aubergine
Spinach
Asparagus
Tarragon
Sage
Broccoli
Bean sprouts
Shallots
Mint
Brussels sprouts
Strawberries
Artichoke
Kale
Radish
Lemongrass
Mustard
Squash
Onions
Sweetcorn
Courgette
Dwarf beans
Chives
Pak choi
Peppers
Celeriac
Oregano
Broad beans
Melon
Rhubarb
Pumpkin
Cornichons
Dill
Runner beans
Endives
Turnip
Rocket

May

May	Plant
In May, seeds can be sown outdoors as the weather is getting warmer. Plant marrow, courgette and sweetcorn in the greenhouse or outdoors later in the month. Outdoors, plant broccoli, Brussels sprouts, cauliflower, kale, peas, lettuce, radish, spinach and swede. **Vegetables** Beetroot and spinach can be thinned out at this time. When the seedlings reach 4cm high, give them water and then thin out so that there is a space of around 10cm between each seedling. Potatoes grow quickly in warm and moist conditions. When they reach 10cm tall, the leafy shoots can be mounded around with soil to their full height; this is known as 'earthing up'. Earthing up potatoes increases the length of underground potato bearing stems. Earth up potatoes by using a hoe to dig up the soil when they reach around 23cm high. Put soil up around the base of the stems of growing broad beans to give them extra support. Runner and French beans seedlings can be planted out towards the end of the month as the weather warms up. Sow outdoors seeds under cloches to help promote germination.	Carrot Cabbage Cress Cauliflower Sweet basil Parsnip Cucumber Parsley Mint Broad beans Tomatoes Chilli peppers Leaf salad Salad onions Leeks Peas Sweet peppers Beetroot Marrow

May is warming up.

PROPAGATION

May | Plant

Marrow, courgette and sweetcorn can be sown in the greenhouse or outdoors at the end of the month, into early June.

Vegetables such as broccoli, Brussels sprouts, cauliflower, kale, peas, lettuce, radish, spinach and swede can be outside or under cloches during early May

Fruit

As the weather warms up keep fruit well-watered in dry spells to help development.

Rhubarb stems which have been kept tightly under jars can be harvested by gripping them firmly at the base, then pulling them sharply away from the crown.

Lay straw between strawberry plants to keep the fruit clean and discourage mould.

General

Guard against any late frost by placing garden fleece over emerging crops such as potatoes. Use polythene or sacking to cover cold frames, while young plants that are in the greenhouse can be covered with newspaper.

Prevent weeds by hoeing your beds once a week.

Many plants are susceptible to attack by aphids, and measures should be taken to bring this common pest under control.

Control aphids with natural and organic sprays

Soap and water: Make a homemade aphid spray by mixing a few tablespoons of a pure liquid soap in a small bucket of water and pour into a spray bottle. Liquid soap contains pure soap with no added perfumes, preservatives or fragrances.

Spray the mixture directly onto the aphids and parts of the plant which are affected. Soak the undersides of leaves where eggs and larvae are often hidden. The soap acts to dissolve the outer layer of aphids and other soft-bodied insects and kills them without harming birds or insects like lacewings, ladybugs or pollinating bees.

Essential oils: Use four to five drops of essential oils such as peppermint, clove, rosemary and thyme, and mix with water in a small spray bottle. Spray on affected plants, on the adult aphids, under the leaves and stalks to coat the aphid larvae and eggs.

Plant

- Lettuce
- Aubergine
- Spinach
- Asparagus
- Tarragon
- Sage
- Broccoli
- Bean sprouts
- Shallots
- Mint
- Brussels sprouts
- Strawberries
- Artichoke
- Kale
- Radish
- Lemongrass
- Mustard
- Squash
- Onions
- Sweetcorn
- Courgette
- Dwarf beans
- Chives
- Pak choi
- Peppers
- Celeriac
- Oregano
- Broad beans
- Melon
- Rhubarb
- Pumpkin
- Cornichons
- Dill
- Runner beans
- Endives
- Turnip
- Coriander
- Purple sprouting broccoli
- Marrow

June	Plant
As June arrives we can but only hope that summer is here. The longer days and the warmer weather make June one of the best times to sow outside. It's also important to prepare the greenhouse to regulate the intensity of the temperature. Sow French, runner and broad beans, peas, squash, sweet corn, outdoor cucumbers and other of your favourite varieties directly into the ground. Plant salad frequently for a continuous crop and new sowings of beetroot, carrots and lettuce, to keep the fresh supplies plentiful throughout the summer. It's important to thin out your seedlings so that the crops are not overcrowded and can flourish. Protect your carrots from pests such as carrot fly, and cabbages from caterpillar damage, by covering them with crop netting. **Vegetables** Plant out greenhouse raised Brussels sprouts, cabbage, celery, courgettes, cucumbers, marrows, runner and French beans. Thin out beetroot, carrots and lettuce rows to continue sowing and prevent over-crowding. In the case of pumpkins, courgettes and marrows, all from the cucurbit family, hand pollinate to encourage good fruit set. These plants can produce lots of leafy growth but this doesn't always mean lots of flowering or fruiting. *June, where summertime hope is in full swing.*	Carrot Cabbage Cress Cauliflower Sweet basil Parsnip Cucumber Parsley Mint Broad beans Tomatoes Chilli peppers Leaf salad Salad onions Leeks Peas Sweet peppers Beetroot Lettuce Marrow

PROPAGATION

June

Cucurbits, with the exception of greenhouse 'all female' cucumber cultivars, produce separate male and female flowers, which require pollination to set fruit. Pollination is usually done by insects and is the transfer of pollen from the male flower to the female flower. There are a few reasons, such as weather or incompatible growing conditions, why plants fail to set despite the plant producing both male and female flowers. The plants could be too young and tiny to sustain fruits, or are hampered during periods of poor and cold weather and low activity of pollinating insects, mainly honeybees.

Hand pollination ensures the transfer of the pollen:
Step 1 – First identify a male flower. They differ from female flowers as they don't have a fruitlet at the base of flower.
Step 2 – Pick off a male flower, then carefully strip the flower petals to revealing the pollen-bearing anthers.
Step 3 – Press the male flower into the centre of the female flowers. One male flower can pollinate multiple female flowers.

If the crop is grown in a greenhouse or cloche with limited insect access, good ventilation with open doors and windows encourages insects. Hand pollination may yet still be necessary.

Protect carrots from carrot fly and cabbages from caterpillar damage by covering the crop with protective mesh.

If you decide to dig up early potatoes take care not to pierce or damage the tubers.

To create a flourishing environment for greenhouse tomatoes, keep the greenhouse well ventilated during the day to equalise the temperature both day and night to help the tomatoes' fruiting. A good tip is to tap the flowers of greenhouse tomatoes to improve pollination.

Fruit

Check fruit bushes and trees for pest and diseases, and treat accordingly.

As new canes of raspberries and blackberries appear, tie to support wires and separate them away from last year's canes for summer flowering and fruit.

Creating a fruit cage or drape netting over soft fruit bushes such as currants, as well as strawberries, helps prevent birds from stripping unprotected plants of their fruit.

Strawberry crops under glass, cloches or straw can now be uncovered so that pollinating insects can do their work.

If strawberries are being grown in a greenhouse open the doors completely.

Trim any new shoots on your gooseberry bushes.

Greenhouse

Hotter days means it's important to water regularly so don't let plants wilt.

Use a high-potash liquid tomato feed to weekly feed cucumbers, capsicums and aubergines.

Manage the greenhouse temperatures on hot days by either using shade netting or a shading paint.

Plant

- Aubergine
- Spinach
- Asparagus
- Tarragon
- Sage
- Broccoli
- Bean sprouts
- Shallots
- Mint
- Brussels sprouts
- Strawberries
- Artichoke
- Kale
- Radish
- Lemongrass
- Mustard
- Squash
- Onions
- Sweetcorn
- Courgette
- Dwarf beans
- Chives
- Pak choi
- Peppers
- Celeriac
- Oregano
- Broad beans
- Melon
- Rhubarb
- Pumpkin
- Cornichons
- Dill
- Runner beans
- Endives
- Turnip

July

July	Plant
The summer is set in and it's time to let the garden bask in the warmth of the sun. Don't let the garden dry out during the hotter months. The best time to water your garden is between 6 am to 10 am, before the heat of the day sets in. This provides the plants plenty of time to drink up and any moisture on the leaves to dry off before nightfall. **Vegetables** Sow spring maturing cabbage, broad and dwarf French beans, carrot, radish, spinach and many more. Keep sowing carrot, lettuce and spinach and plant out pot-grown sweetcorn in blocks instead of rows, spacing them around 45cm apart. Harvest young and tender beetroot and other crops. Pick runner bean, French beans and courgettes regularly to encourage further cropping. Cut away side shoots on tomatoes and crop the plants when 4–5 trusses have grown out. Feed them often with a high potash liquid fertiliser. Do not allow plants to dry out as it can cause blossom end rot. This is signified by dark blotches on the ends of aubergine, tomato and pepper. It can be alarming, but it does not mean the end of the crop. It is caused by lack of calcium in the fruits. It is possible to be able to protect subsequent fruits from blossom end rot by adjusting the frequency of watering.	Carrot Cabbage Cress Cauliflower Sweet basil Parsnip Cucumber Parsley Mint Broad beans Tomatoes Chilli peppers Leaf salad Salad onions Leeks Peas Sweet peppers Beetroot Lettuce

July gardens bask in sunshine.

PROPAGATION

July

Don't let your onions go short of water as this will affect the size of crop. In dry conditions its best to make sure they are watered once or twice a week; and weed regularly.

Check on second early potatoes to make sure they have grown into a good size. Do this by examining one of the plants and if they are not quite big enough leave them a little longer. It is important to water regularly every week.

Sowing spring maturing cabbage, broad bean and dwarf French beans can still be made until the middle of the month.

Regularly pick runner and French beans and courgettes to encourage further cropping.

Stems cut from herbs, such as thyme and sage, can produce fresh healthy new stems which will root and create fresh new plants

Fruit

Strawberries, raspberries, redcurrants, cherries and rhubarb should be ready for harvest so enjoy your pickings.

Cut surplus strawberry runners close to the plants.

Prune established plums and apricots.

Tie to supports any new canes of blackberries and loganberries.

If you have protected your fruit bushes with netting over them, make sure no birds are trapped in the nets.

Greenhouse

As the July sun beats down keep watering your plants daily and include feeding them weekly.

Plant

Aubergine
Spinach
Asparagus
Tarragon
Sage
Broccoli
Bean sprouts
Shallots
Mint
Brussels sprouts
Strawberries
Artichoke
Kale
Radish
Lemongrass
Mustard
Squash
Onions
Sweetcorn
Courgette
Dwarf beans
Chives
Pak choi
Peppers
Celeriac
Oregano
Broad beans
Melon
Rhubarb
Pumpkin
Cornichons
Dill
Runner beans
Endives
Turnip
Chicory
Chinese cabbage

GROW YOUR OWN FOOD

AUGUST

August	Plant
August is when the new generation of adult ladybirds emerge from the pupae. Not only are ladybirds a delightful decorative addition to the garden they are also a gardener's soldier, because they are a natural predator of aphids such as greenfly, blackfly and whitefly. To deploy the ladybirds in pest control, collect from your garden and place it in your greenhouse, fruit trees or anywhere there may be flies. The ladybird will make itself at home and feast on aphids. August is a time to plan ahead for your autumn and winter veg so start sowing cabbages, chard, radishes and turnips, but also keep your salads fresh with more plantings. Cover cabbages and chard with a cloche to protect them for a ready supply of homegrown veg in time for winter.	Onion Radish Lettuce Cress Salad onion Spinach Beetroot Turnip Onion Pak choi Broad beans

August is bountiful.

PROPAGATION

August

Just in case you have decided to sow any more vegetables this year, sow in some green manure seeds to protect the nutrients in the soil during winter.

Vegetables

August is a time to pinch out your vegetables. Pinching plants is a term which refers to a form of pruning which promotes branching on the plant. By pinching out a plant, you are removing the main stem, forcing the plant to grow two new stems from the leaf nodes which are below the pinch or pruned point. The purpose is to force the plant into a fuller form so the plant to grows twice as many stems. For plants such as herbs, pinching back encourages the plant to grow more of their desirable leaves. We also pinch plants to keep them compact. By pinching the plant, it makes the plant focus on re-growing lost stems instead of height. Pinching a plant is a relatively simple procedure. The term derives from the pinch by your fingers to block the new growth at the end of the stem. You can also use a sharp pair of pruning shears to pinch the ends. If possible, pinch the stem above the leaf nodes.

The tips of cucumber side shoots should be pinched out just two leaves beyond any fruit that may be developing.

Water tomato plants weekly with a high potash tomato fertiliser feed and keep them well watered. The side shoots on tomatoes should be pinched out regularly and the main shoots tied to the supports.

The tips of cucumber side shoots should be pinched out just two leaves beyond any developing fruit. If any old fruit is left on the plants this will affect further flowering so remember to pick cucumbers on a regular basis.

Pinch out the tips of any climbing shoots of runner beans if they reach the top of their supports.

Plant Japanese bulb onions such as the senshyu semi-globe yellow outdoors from mid to late August for harvesting in July.

If you have the space then sow some spring cabbage, Chinese cabbage, winter lettuce and radish.

Dig up main crop potatoes and either use immediately or store for harvest in September or early October.

If you are digging up your potatoes, you could replace them with late season potatoes for second crop in October.

If conditions are hot and humid your potato crop may become victim to potato blight. Blight is a fungal disease caused by spores of *Phytophthora infestans*. The spores are spread by the wind and then contaminate potato tubers in the soil. It's better to prevent blight as is it is difficult to cure. In order to try and prevent blight, plant healthy, disease-free seed potatoes from a reputable supplier. Early crops, harvested before the worst of the blight season, have less chance of being exposed. Select an open planting site with good airflow. Keep the plants spaced apart so better airflow means the foliage will dry quickly following rain, which reduces the spread of blight between plants. In dry weather, water plants in the morning, at the base of the plant only, so that any moisture on the leaves can evaporate during the day. You should check the plants regularly and be prepared to act quickly if you should notice any signs of blight. If only a few leaves are affected, you can remove them and dispose of them safely.

Plant

Chilli pepper
Bean sprouts
Watercress
Cabbage
Carrot
Kale

August — Plant

Crop rotation helps stop an accumulation of disease spores in the ground, and prevents infected plants growing out of potato tubers that may have been missed during last year's harvest. It's important to vigilantly dig up every last potato so blight has nowhere to hide during the winter.

Spray potato crops with a protective fungicide before signs of blight appear. Start from June, especially if the weather's wet. Spray again after a few weeks to protect new growth.

You could try this homemade Bordeaux formula:
- Mix 1 x 450g of slaked / hydrated lime in 4 litres of water
- Mix 1 x 450g of copper sulphate crystals/powder in 4 litres of water
- Fill a container with 8 litres of water and add 950ml of copper sulphate solution and 950ml of lime solution.

The Bordeaux formula is now ready to use.

Regularly pick small, tender courgettes by carefully cutting them off at the base. Watch out for the prickly leaves, and perhaps wear gloves to protect your hands.

Any flowering, fruit bearing or plants with pods on them must be watered well.

Fruit

During dry spells keep plants well-watered and weeds under control by hoeing around the bases.

Summer fruited raspberries need cutting back once they have finished cropping. Tie up new canes to supports and get rid of any spare ones.

Secure runners of new strawberry plants into pots of compost or soil so they root. The foliage should be removed just above the crown of each plant, remembering to clear away any debris.

Tie grapevines to supports.

Prune back the main shoots and side shoots of gooseberries to five leaves, which encourages fruiting shoots to be produced for next season.

PROPAGATION

SEPTEMBER

September	Plant
This is the time to sow your winter vegetables and keep your garden productive. Plant salad onions which will be ready for early spring, broccoli for the first harvests next year, and winter lettuce and radishes. Between September up until October this is when your cold frame and greenhouse come into their own, as there is a range of vegetables that can be planted. However, if you intend to sow your September seeds outside, then cover with perforated polythene to protect them.	Onion Radish Lettuce Cress Salad onion Spinach Beetroot

September harvest is rich and varied.

GROW YOUR OWN FOOD

September | Plant

Vegetables

Plant spring cabbage into their winter growing positions.

For a plentiful supply of herbs during the winter, pot up basil, marjoram, mint, oregano and parsley plants to be grown on a windowsill.

Why not pot some cut-and-come again salad varieties to be grown indoors as well?

Onion sets of an over-wintering variety can be planted from the middle of the month.

Sow winter lettuce

Dig up main crop potatoes and allow to dry prior to storing in wooden trays in a dark, cool, frost-free place.

Any remaining crops need to be picked regularly, ensuring they are always fresh and tender, and vegetables, such as courgettes and beans, aren't as tasty if left too long.

Keep watering tomatoes and chillies in greenhouses during late summer.

Celery plants reaching required size can be lifted carefully with a hand fork.

It's also time to grow autumn-planting shallots and onions, and they will be ready to harvest June to July (shallots until September) the next year.

Fruit

To grow new blackberry plants, plant the tips of any shoots that have developed this year into the soil, as they will quickly form roots and new shoots will develop next spring. Once they have rooted separate them and plant them where you plan to grow them.

Prevent wasp damage to early fruiting apples by hanging wasp traps in the branches of the trees.

Pick fruit from these early ripening apple trees once they are sweet enough to eat as they won't keep.

Prune all peach shoots that have carried peaches so that newly formed ones can be tied to ones formed this year and these will flower next spring.

Regularly pick crops of raspberries, blackberries and other autumn-fruiting varieties and make sure they are covered with netting to keep birds away.

Plant
- Turnip
- Onion
- Pak choi
- Broad beans
- Chilli pepper
- Bean sprouts
- Watercress
- Cabbage
- Carrot
- Kale

PROPAGATION

OCTOBER

October	Plant
The nights are drawing in but there are still vegetables that can be sown, such as basil, broad beans, broccoli, cabbage, cauliflower, kale, onions and radish. October means that there is still plenty of work to be done, such as clearing the ground and weeding. **Vegetables** This is the perfect time to grow some autumn-planting garlic. Plant your garlic cloves from October to January and they should be ready to harvest May to July the following year. Autumn-planting onion and shallot sets can also be planted in a well-drained, sunny position, up to the end of November. Towards the end of the month sow broad beans in a sheltered area. Dig up any remaining root crops such as carrots, beetroot and potatoes. Cut back asparagus to ground level. **Fruit** Prepare the ground for planting soft fruit. Choose a well-drained, sunny position which is not impacted by late frosts. Dig over the area, dig in well-rotted farmyard manure or garden compost and remove any weed roots. Set up supports for cane fruits such as raspberries. Pick the berries of late fruiting varieties of blackberries	Onions Cress Broad beans Salad leaves Spinach Salad onion Radish Broccoli Carrots Kale Salad onions Cauliflower Lettuce

October is the time to clear the ground.

GROW YOUR OWN FOOD

NOVEMBER

November

The cold winter days of November are upon us. If you are planning to sow in these months, the seeds will need some protection. You can sow early mangetout, winter lettuce, broad bean, pea and delicious sprouting seed varieties.

Vegetables

Sow broad beans outdoors under the protection of cloches.

Plant suitable varieties of garlic until the middle of the month.

Protect crowns of globe artichoke from frost by wrapping straw around the base of the plants.

Sow the early variety of mangetout pea under cloches this month.

Bring indoors potted up herbs for the winter.

Lift and divide overcrowded clumps of chives.

For a continuous supply of lettuce crops during winter, plant varieties in pots, borders or growbags and grow on in a warm greenhouse.

Plant

Cress
Broad beans
Peas
Bean sprouts
Kale
Lettuce

November nights are drawing in.

PROPAGATION

November — Plant

Some winter vegetables such as kale, hardy broccoli, turnips and spinach are hardy enough to survive a few frosts, not including extreme frosts, without being covered. If a frost is predicted, crops such as lettuces, chard, beets and radishes are less hardy, so it's wise to cover your rows with a garden cloth or tarp. Protect individual plants by covering them with pots or plastic bottles with the bottoms cut off. If the forecast is for an overnight frost, cover your plants as soon as the sun goes down. Winterising crops such as garlic and onions should be mulched with straw or wood chip before frosts set in so that the bulbs remain warm enough underground.

Another solution to protect plants from the cold is to build a wall around your vegetable beds to shield them from sharp, cold winds, especially if you live in a windy area. Use piled up bricks for a smaller patch, or build a fence and wrap plastic or agricultural cloth around it for larger plots.

Cold frames protect your plants from cold nights as well as help them warm up during the day. It is a bottomless case with a transparent glass or plastic cover, which is placed over your plants. On sunny days the sun shines through the clear cover creating a mini greenhouse, at the same time the cover retains the heat and keeps the cold at bay during the night or on days that the temperature drops below freezing. You can buy a cold frame, or make your own out of recycled wood and old windowpanes, or a strong plastic. Cold frames work well with raised beds, as they can be made to fit the bed and are easily stored away during warmer months.

Fruit

Plant soft fruit in prepared ground covered with well-rotted manure or garden compost.

Prune back blackberry canes to soil level and tie new ones into their place. Long canes need to be trained back down towards the soil. Bury tips of canes in the soil to root which will then form new plants.

Pick ripe apples and, depending on the variety, they can either be eaten or stored in a cool, dry place for later use.

Wrap glue bands around fruit trees.

General

Wash down your greenhouse on a warm day to remove any algae and grime which has built up, hindering light reaching the plants inside.

Close vents in the greenhouse by mid-afternoon to retain warmth.

Any plants that are being over-wintered under glass need to be checked regularly to ensure they are healthy and free from disease.

Remove any dead flowers or discoloured leaves.

Clean and disinfect pots and trays ready for next season.

Start planning your garden for next year, and think about ordering plants and seeds early to avoid disappointment.

December

December	Plant
You can sow onions and peas, and broad beans and delicious, vitamin-packed sprouting seeds too. If the ground isn't frozen, vacant areas in the vegetable plot can be dug ready for sowing and planting in spring. **Vegetables** Sow broad beans outdoors or under cloches. Sow large onions during December and early January in preparation for transplanting the young plants outdoors in spring.	Cress Beans Peas Onions Kale Lettuce

December is filled with thoughts of spring.

PROPAGATION

December — Plant

Lift back chicory roots by cutting back tops and potting up, which will make them produce blanched, tender chicons with whitened leafy shoots. Three roots should be contained in a 25cm pot, and to prevent the light getting through place another upturned pot on top.

Fruit
Plant dormant soft fruit such as currants, gooseberries, raspberries, blackberries and tayberries.

Currants – extra plants can be grown from hardwood cuttings taken from existing healthy bushes. The cuttings should be 25–30cm in length, then dug in to about half their depth.

Blackcurrants – prune back established plants allowing the young wood, which will bear most of the fruit, to flourish in the spring. Keep all the buds that are intact, unless they are redcurrants, where only the top four should be left. Remove all the others.

Gooseberries – take cuttings around 25–30cm in length, then dig in to about half their depth.

Rhubarb – lift out clumps, and pot them up in large boxes for forcing and store them in the greenhouse or shed. Cover the roots with moist compost, then keep the light out with the support of a frame. Place black polythene over the top.

Greenhouses
Keep the gutters clear of any leaves or debris.
    Check heaters are working
    Keep an eye out for pests which may overwinter on plants. Small infestations of red spider mite, greenfly and whitefly can quickly spread. To prevent future problems, control now by either spraying, removing them from the leaves or disposing of any plants that are infected.

CHAPTER 4

Seeing the Light

Holistic thinking helps with garden maintenance.

The look of a vegetable garden is not a priority. Your primary concern is planting vegetables in their optimal growing conditions and creating enough room for paths and space for working. Make sure you make your paths wide enough to get your wheelbarrow through.

As we have previously discussed you don't usually plant your vegetable garden all at once. Some vegetables only produce for a limited time so can be sown in staggered plantings to extend the harvest. You can make the most of your vegetable garden space in different ways. You can choose small, or dwarf, plant varieties, or vining plants, which can be trained upward. Another option is to mix sun-loving plants and shade-tolerant plants so that the sun-loving plants offer shade for the latter.

Most vegetables can be grown in containers and pots. It enables you to control the soil and drainage and ensures the soil is good quality. The containers can be situated in the sunlight, and moved around to follow the sun. Larger vegetables can't be cramped into a pot so it's important to make sure they have enough room to grow within the container. The downside is they need more water and food than in-ground plants.

A vegetable garden needs regular maintenance. Some tasks, like staking and mulching, need to be done early in the season. Watering and weeding are an ongoing task.

Pest control is an essential part of vegetable gardening. The key is to stay on top of the situation and take the appropriate steps when necessary rather than retrospectively spraying toxins onto your food. This is known as Integrated Pest Management, or IPM.

Having your food and plants being attacked by pests and diseases can be very annoying. Monitoring your garden regularly draws attention to any problems early enough to prevent major damage and gives you time to act. This list will help you learn about common pests and diseases and how to identify them.

Common garden pests

Aphids
From the insect family Aphididae, aphids are small sucking insects. There are roughly 5,000 different species, with several hundred posing a problem for agriculture and gardening. Adult aphids are the shape of pear-drops and about 10mm in length. The most common aphids are the light green ones (pear aphids), but aphids can be a variety of colours such as pink, white, grey and black. Further, when colonies are established, winged aphids can appear and fly to infect new plants. Juvenile aphids (nymphs) are simply smaller versions of the adults.

Aphids are small sucking insects.

Aphid infestations damage plants and can develop quickly. The insects rapidly travel from one plant to another. Outside, aphid colonies are tended by ants that protect them from predators. Ants feed on aphid honeydew, which is sweet liquid secreted by aphids as they feed on plant sap. Inside, aphids fly and crawl between plants, building colonies.

Aphids suck sap from new growth on plants which causes damage. They attach in clusters to the soft, green stems. If untreated the plant will begin to drop leaves and the honeydew secreted by aphids can cause the growth of sooty mould and fungus.

Preventing and dealing with aphids

Healthy plants are less susceptible to aphid infestation. Keeping your plants healthy is less likely to attract aphids. However, should you discover aphids on your plants here are some solutions:

Wash them off: If the infestation is light, flush the aphids from your plants with a stream of water and also knock them off with your fingers.

Dip in water: If the plant has fragile foliage which is too fine to be sprayed, you can dip the entire plant in water to get rid of them. Simply, turn it upside down and dip the foliage into a pot of fresh room-temperature water.

Spray with insecticidal soap: There are several ways to make an insecticidal soap. It's better to select ingredients which are not full of perfumes or dyes. Take 250ml of oil, any type, such as vegetable or rapeseed, to one tablespoon of pure liquid soap. Mix two teaspoons of the soap solution to 250ml of warm water and put into a spray bottle. Mix only what you need to spray on the day. Spray onto the plants, concentrating on the undersides of the leaves. This spray can be used on soft bodied insects such as aphids, whiteflies, spider mites and mealybugs. Insecticidal soaps can also be beneficial in getting rid of sooty mould, honeydew and other leaf fungi.

Make your own homemade insect spray: To make your own spray, put 1 garlic bulb, 1 small onion, and 1 teaspoon of cayenne pepper in a food processor or blender and process into a paste. Mix the paste into 1 litre of water and steep for 1 hour. Sieve the mixture and add 1 tablespoon of liquid dish soap. Mix well. Add to a spray bottle. Spray onto the plants, concentrating on the undersides of the leaves. If refrigerated, the mixture can be stored for up to one week.

Rubbing alcohol: Coat the aphids with a swab dipped in rubbing alcohol. It can be a time-consuming task.

Cut away: Remove the sections of the plant which are heavily infested and throw them away.

Hang fly tape: Sheets or strips of sticky flypaper hung above your plants will trap any insects flying around.

Cabbage white butterflies

Protect your cabbages and other brassicas by preventing attacks from cabbage white butterflies. The white butterflies don't cause any actual damage, but their offspring do. They lay their eggs on the underside of the leaves, and the caterpillars demolish every millimetre of leaf, leaving just the stalks, or at best a munched crop covered in caterpillars and their caterpillar faecal matter. They'll eat any brassica, so cabbages, broccoli, kale, cauliflower and sprouts are on the menu.

The white butterfly is harmless but the caterpillars demolish.

In the UK there are two species of cabbage white butterfly: these are the small white (*Pieris rapae*) and the large white (*Pieris brassicae*). They are similar in appearance. They are both white with a pale green hue on the undersides of their wings, and grey-black spots on the upper wings. Of the two, the large white can reap more havoc and will spoil a crop given the opportunity.

Prevention is better than cure. Protecting your crops is the best way to stop the butterflies reaching them and laying eggs on them. Butterflies are on the wing from February to November, so use a mesh as a protective barrier. Assemble frames or hoops to support it, ensuring that it reaches the soil and is sealed all around so the butterflies can't get through any gaps.

If you need to remove the covering to water or weed and then replace, check that you haven't trapped a butterfly inside, which could create carnage.

The pale green small white caterpillars are sneaky and well camouflaged. Regularly check your plants and remove any eggs or caterpillars that you discover. The satiated caterpillar is full of mustard oil, which is a cunning self-defence mechanism as this is unpalatable to predators, which means they are left alone by birds. Holes in cabbage leaves are an identifier of feeding caterpillars. Hand-remove adults and look for eggs on the undersides of the leaves.

You can, however, use predatory nematodes to control the caterpillars. Nematodes are microscopic creatures, which behave as parasites on other insects and can be an organic solution. To kill the caterpillars the nematode releases bacteria into the host's body and then eats the host. When you spot the caterpillars spray the nematodes on to the plants and then twice more later to control further hatchings.

Apply nematode based solutions to the soil with a watering can or hose end feeder to control soil-based pests. Alternatively, apply with a sprayer to control, and continue to apply while the pests are active. The soil temp needs to be 12°C.

Nemotodes can also be used to treat the following pests:

Carrot root fly
Carrot fly is a pest which targets carrots, parsnips, celery, celeriac and parsley. In contrast to its name it is a weak flier and hangs around the edges of fields and gardens, identifying the target vegetable by scent. Attacks occur more often in old established gardens where the population develops year on year. Eggs are laid in the soil next to the plant, and as they hatch out the 9mm yellow/white maggots burrow into the roots. The maggots remain in the ground over winter, pupate, and in the spring the life cycle begins once more. Two additional generations can appear throughout the year. Early in the planting season is when the attacks are worse, but following attacks can also occur in the autumn and winter in mild seasons.

Application
Pour the solution liberally around roots of the plants or where the fly is present, either with a watering can with a coarse rose or a hose end feeder. Drench the rows and around the plants. The pests will be located next to the stems and roots of plants.
Covers up to 60 sq.m.
Apply: April to July.
How often: Apply fortnightly during the growing season.

Cabbage root fly

Cabbage root fly targets all brassicas; cabbages, cauliflowers, broccoli, calabrese, Brussels sprouts, kale and root vegetables such as turnip, swede and radishes. It has a rapid lifecycle so the cabbage root fly poses a problem during the season until it overwinters as a pupa. From mid spring to early autumn there are three generations of fly, laying their eggs in the soil close to the stems of the plants. Out of the eggs hatch white legless maggots, up to 9mm in length and which feed on the roots. It takes around three weeks for the maggots to grow fully into a small brown pupa, and an extra week for the egg-laying fly to emerge.

Application

Pour the solution liberally around roots of the plants or where the fly is present, either with a watering can with a coarse rose or a hose end feeder. Drench the rows and around the plants. The pests will be located next to the stems and roots of plants.
Covers up to 60 sq.m.
Apply: April to July.
How often: Apply fortnightly during the growing season.

Cutworms

Cutworms are caterpillars of various moth species which live in the soil. The moths lay around 30–50 eggs on leaves and stems. Cutworm caterpillars grow up to 40mm long with a creamy-brown, greenish-brown or greyish-white colour, feeding on many types of vegetables, fruit and, a few months later, they pupate in the soil. In August or September a second generation is born to feed, and to overwinter during the colder weather.

Application

Pour the solution liberally around roots of the plants or where the fly is present, either with a watering can with a coarse rose or a hose end feeder. Drench the rows and around the plants. The pests will be located next to the stems and roots of plants.
Covers up to 60 sq.m.
Apply: April to July.
How often: Apply fortnightly during the growing season.

Onion fly

Unsurprisingly, the onion is the most vulnerable plant to the onion fly. However, other alliums such as leeks, shallots and garlic can also be attacked. Onion flies lay white maggots, which are up to 8mm long and are laid near the base of the plant or in the leaves. From the spring till late summer, they create up to three generations per year, with the final generation overwintering as pupae in the soil.

Application

Pour the solution liberally around roots of the plants or where the fly is present, either with a watering can with a coarse rose or a hose end feeder. Drench the rows and around the plants. The pests will be located next to the stems and roots of plants.
Covers up to 60 sq.m.
Apply: April to July.
How often: Apply fortnightly during the growing season.

Leatherjackets

The crane fly or daddy longlegs larvae are called leatherjackets and are about 2.5cm long and greyish black in colour. Around the end of August, the advent of adult daddy longlegs in your garden is an indicator they will soon be laying eggs, which then hatch about two weeks later. The young start to feed continuously during the winter so they can devour the roots in the spring.

Application

Pour the solution liberally around roots of the plants or where the fly is present, either with a watering can with a coarse rose or a hose end feeder. Apply to the entire soil area.

Covers up to 60 sq.m.

Apply: April to July.

How often: Apply fortnightly during the growing season.

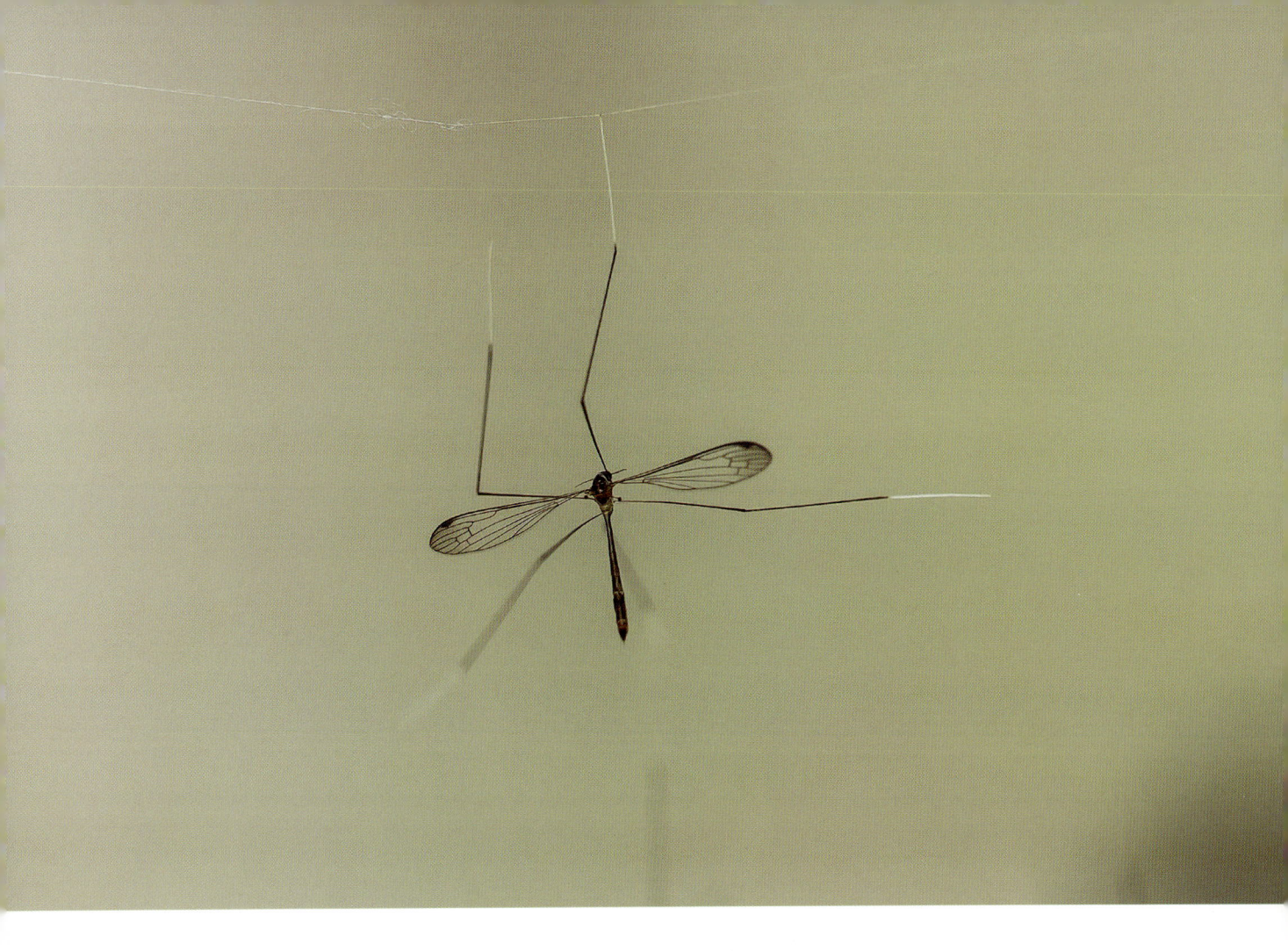

Ants

There are four stages of ant development: egg, larvae, pupae (or cocoon in some species) and adult. There are three main castes, each with different roles: workers, queens and males. The ant life span varies species by species from a few weeks to many years. Of the 50 species of ants found in the United Kingdom not all are native. The problem species of ants are: *Lasius niger*, the common black garden ant; *Lasius flavius*, the yellow meadow ant; and *Myrmica* species, the red ants.

There are 50 species of ant in the UK.

Application
Pour the solution liberally around roots of the plants or where the ant is present, either with a watering can with a coarse rose or a hose end feeder.
Covers up to 60 sq.m.
Apply: April to July.
How often: Regular applications are required to control the ants.
Notes: Ants move their nests if nematodes are applied. Apply to the entire soil area or to individual ant nests directly.

Sciarid
At about 3–4mm long, with slender bodies, sciarid fly or fungus gnats are greyish-brown flies. They loiter on the soil surface and the leaves of potted plants. The 5mm long maggots are white with a black head. They live in the soil and cause to damage vegetable seedlings, or the base of soft cuttings.

Application
Pour the solution liberally around roots of the plants or where the fly is present, either with a watering can with a coarse rose or a hose end feeder.
Covers up to 60 sq.m.
Apply: April to July.
How often: Regular applications are required to control the flies.
Notes: Predominantly a greenhouse pest so pour onto the soil in pots, growing bags or open soil.

Gooseberry sawfly

The gooseberry sawfly targets gooseberries, red and white currants, stripping them of all leaves. There are three species and all of them are around 20mm long and pale green. Two of the species are heavily marked with black spots. Mid to late spring is when they attack, with several generations in a season.

Application

Use a pump sprayer. Wet areas before applying and then spray the pests on the plants. Pests not directly sprayed will not be controlled. Avoid applying in direct sunlight.

Covers up to 60 sq.m.

Apply: As soon as gooseberry sawfly appears, apply weekly until all pests have hatched out.

How often: At least three applications to control all pests hatching out.

Notes: It is essential that the application has contact with the fly.

Thrips

Thrips suck the sap of leaves which causes discoloration on the surface. The adults are 1–2mm long with yellow and brown, black, or black and white colourings. They lay their eggs onto leaves, buds and petals, which hatch out into larvae and pupate. Generation is quick and it can only be two weeks, so breaking the life cycle is key to controlling this pest. It is worth noting that plant virus diseases can be spread by some of the species.

Application

A pump sprayer is best way to apply the nematodes. Spray areas with water before applying and then spray the nematodes onto the plants. If the pests are not directly sprayed they will not be controlled. Do not apply in direct sunlight.

Covers up to 60 sq.m.

Apply: Apply when the thrip is present. Apply weekly until all pests have hatched out.

How often: A minimum of three applications are recommended to prevent all pests hatching out.

Notes: It is essential that the application has direct contact with the thrip.

Codling moth
The Codling moth caterpillar is small and white with a brown head. It burrows into the fruit of apples and pears in mid to late summer. By the time the fruit is ripe they have finished feeding and drop on to the bark of the tree and the soil immediately underneath to overwinter, ready for the moths to emerge in the late spring.

Application
A pump sprayer is best way to apply the nematodes. Spray areas with water before applying and then spray the nematodes onto the plants. Then apply to the trunk, main branches and soil beneath the canopy.
Covers up to 16 trees.
Apply: Throughout September or October.
How often: A minimum of three weekly applications are recommended to prevent all pests hatching out.
Notes: The nematodes control the overwintering stages and can provide protection for the next year.

Other pests and quick fixes

Spider mites
Sever spider mite infestation causes the leaves to dry out and die. The solution is to spray with horticultural soap to control spider mites.

Squash bugs
Squash bug eggs hatch into nymphs on the undersides of these leaves. Remove any damaged leaves and look for adults.

Tomato hornworms caterpillars

The tomato hornworm caterpillar is the larvae of the five-spotted hawk moth. Despite their aesthetic appearance in either stage, the hornworms enjoy munching on the leaves of tomato and pepper plants. However, the hornworms blend in beautifully with the foliage and stalks, and you might only notice them once they have caused damage. The hornworm is a reasonable size, and the simplest way to remove it is to lift from the plant and get rid of it.

As always prevention is better than cure. Keep an eye on the underside of leaves in the spring and remove the eggs and hornworms or smaller caterpillars by hand. Throw them in soapy water to kill them.

In spring and summer, the moths lay their eggs on and under tomato leaves, which hatch into caterpillars. Removing the eggs and caterpillars regularly by hand, should prevent damage to your plants, leaves and tomatoes.

Whiteflies

Whiteflies can cause wilting, stunting and death by feeding off plants, sucking them dry. They are related to aphids and mealybugs, with a population that can expand rapidly. Monitoring your plants is key to keeping the population down. Don't introduce infected plants into your garden. If you discover an infected plant wash it off with a blast of water using a hose, or alternatively, dip the plant into a bucket of water.

Wireworms

Wireworms can often be found in most types of soil all year round. They feed on the roots of plants, impeding growth and weakening the plant. If you think wireworms are in your soil there are some techniques which can limit their destructiveness.

In May and June, when they hatch, turnover the soil which exposes them to hungry birds.

Use pieces of potato or sweet potato as a decoy. Thread a piece of raw potato with string and bury it near the affected soil. After a week pull it back up and check for the presence of wireworms. Get rid of the potato piece, wireworms and all. If crops are infected, remove them and destroy them after harvesting to limit overwintering.

Cucumber beetles

Cucumber beetles eat roots, leaves, and flowers, and by doing so transmit bacterial wilt disease. Although the damage isn't enough to kill the plants, the bacterial wilt often kills the flowers, which results in a loss of fruits. Beginning with one leaf wilting, bacterial wilt can spread rapidly. This is indicated by a sticky, white sap-like substance which exudes from snapped stems. Bacterial wilt is a serious disease for cucumbers and muskmelons, and on less of a scale, also for squash. In order to prevent damage by cucumber beetles buy wilt-resistant plants and keep them off the ground by using a trellis or struts.

Leaf spot

Septoria leaf spot is a common disease of the tomato plant, but can also spread to potatoes and aubergines. The disease is caused by a fungus known as *Septoria lycopersici*, which won't always kill your tomato plants. However, it can do some pretty severe damage and take over the whole plant, preventing fruit production.

Wind or water transports the fungus spores, which lay on top of the soil until the right conditions come along. In warm, damp conditions, the spores attach to the underside of leaves. Early spotting can mean the plants can be saved.

Check the leaves regularly and often, because this is where the tiny circular grey and brown spots symptoms will first appear. As the disease progresses they grow larger, merging together. They could also appear on the stems and blossoms but rarely directly affect the plant fruit. If untreated, leaf spot causes all of the leaves to dry out and fall off the plant. Without leaves, the plant ceases to produce tomatoes.

How to treat leaf spot

As soon as you identify leaf spot remove all infected leaves immediately. To prevent further spread, wash your hands so you don't spread it on to uninfected plants. Sanitise any tools that you have used on the plant.

Once you have removed the diseased leaves, improve air circulation around the plants. Instead of overhead watering or watering the soil directly, try drip irrigation and keep the leaves as dry as possible. Weed regularly and mulch around the base of the plant. Crop rotation by alternating where you plant tomatoes, and never planting tomatoes in a place where tomatoes, potatoes, or aubergine have previously grown helps prevent leaf spot.

However, if you don't catch it quick enough, leaf removal doesn't stop the spread. Organic fungicides can help treat and prevent fungal infections, such as leaf spot. Fungicides with copper and potassium bicarbonate help manage fungal disease and contain it. Begin spraying as soon as the symptoms appear. Treat as directed by the fungicide label.

Let's talk about slugs

Slugs are a gardener's peril. They are often hard to spot, hiding under leaves in the damp regions of your garden and devouring plants along the way, in particular wreaking havoc on vegetable and berry crops by eating both the leaves and the fruit. Damage often happens surreptitiously and can often occur before you even know your garden is under attack.

There are a few options, and even preferences, for slug management.

Slugs wreak havoc in the garden.

When is the best time to stop slugs in their tracks? Slugs can be treated any time during the growing season. Often evidence of their presence is apparent but finding them can be tricky as they camouflage against the brown soil and stow away in damp, dark places during the day. They leave signs so look out for holes in leaves, bites taken out of fruit, slimy trails or little white eggs in the ground. Once you have identified that you have slugs it's time to act.

Slug prevention methods

Equipment
Gardening gloves
Spray bottle
Garden spreader
Dust mask

Materials
Salt
Water
Bottle of beer
Diatomaceous earth
Organic commercial slug bait

SEEING THE LIGHT

The salt method
This method is an effective way of killing slugs and keeping them at bay.

Combine a strong solution of salt and water into a spray bottle. It doesn't have to be precise ratios but just make sure the salt is very prevalent in the mix. Spray. As the night falls venture out into the garden as this when the slugs begin to emerge. Spray the slugs. The salt solution will dehydrate the slugs within hours. Wash away the salt spray. In the morning flush away any residual salt spray with fresh water from your plants to prevent salt damage.

The beer method
This method uses bottled beer as a homemade trap to attract the slugs. It can take a few days to work and also means donating beer to slugs instead of drinking it. Open the beer, and pour most of the contents into a glass for you to drink. There needs to be just enough beer left in the bottle so that when you lay it on its side beer won't spill out. Lay a few of these bottle traps.

During the day, place the bottles in various locations around your garden. Lay each bottle on its side, press it into the ground so the bottle opening rests on the surface.

During the night the slugs are lured into the bottles because they're attracted to the beer. Once inside, they will drown in the remaining beer.

The bottles need to remain in place for several nights. A few days later, when they are full, remove them, empty out the dead slugs, and recycle. Repeat if necessary.

The earth method

The use of diatomaceous earth for pest control is a popular method with some gardeners. Diatomaceous earth consists of the fossilised remains (silica) of small aquatic organisms known as diatoms. Slugs ingest the silica, which then dries them up from the inside. The earth, however, is nontoxic to humans and pets.

Rain will stop play, though. It is important to wait for a dry day to treat your garden. Check the forecast and that there is a dry spell for at least 24 hours. Sprinkle the earth. Protect your hands with gardening gloves and your face with a dust mask, and sprinkle the diatomaceous earth in various places around your garden. Make sure that you don't sprinkle it on the leaves of the plants. Wait a few days for the slugs to eat the diatomaceous earth. Repeat if necessary on another dry day.

The organic slug bait method

If you need to use treatments purchase organic slug bait. Many include iron phosphate, which is toxic to slugs but much less dangerous for humans and pets.

It is important to wait for a dry day to treat your garden. Check the forecast and that there is a dry spell for at least 24 hours. With gardening gloves on, fill your garden spreader with the granules. Follow the product's guidelines regarding the volume required for the area you're treating. Wait a few days for the slugs to eat the bait. Repeat if necessary on another dry day.

The poultry method

If you keep chickens and other animals you can use them to naturally control slugs. If you let your birds roam free they will eat slugs and other pests that accumulate in the garden. You can even give your chickens a taste for slugs by tossing some inside their area. Although be warned: chickens like to scratch and eat veggies. If you are not careful they might tuck into your fruits and veggies too.

Garden maintenance tips

Vegetables are less forgiving of neglect than ornamental plants or even fruit. Vegetable plants use an incredible amount of energy blooming and producing fruit which never reaches fruition as far as the plants are concerned. The vegetable plant sets fruit to produce seed, but we usually harvest the vegetables before the seeds are fully formed. This is stressful for vegetable plants, so it's important to nourish them for the health, vigour and strength to continue production. Neglecting your vegetable plants can result in reduced yields and inferior vegetables and increased likelihood of pest problems.

Watering

To your vegetables water is as important as sunlight. They need at least 5cm per week, every week, and more if the weather is extremely hot. If you don't water them frequently, and when needed, then you can damage the plant. Without regular water, vegetables will not fill out and some, like tomatoes, will crack open if suddenly plumped up with water after struggling without for a while.

As the weather is very unpredictable, if you have the means it is worth setting up an irrigation system for a vegetable garden or greenhouse. The new component systems are easy to install and affordable. The water is used more efficiently too, because it goes directly to the plant's root, with less lost to evaporation. Some systems can connect with WIFI so you can turn on and off remotely. This can come in very handy if you are on holiday or away from home. I had an app-controlled irrigation system and I was able to water my tomatoes remotely, which was very useful.

When planning your planting it is important to think about how easily you can water your plants. I once installed big water bowsers near my raised beds, which I filled up with the hose so that I could easily water the beds when my mains water pressure was very weak.

It's important to consider how readily and easily you can water your vegetables. Is your hose long enough? Is your water pressure strong enough? Are you going to use a watering can? How many times will you need to refill it? How far away is the water source? Is it easy to do? It's important to make sure watering isn't a hindrance which creates obstacles, especially during the summer months when it can be required daily, or sometimes every morning and evening.

Water is the elixir of life.

Maintain your vegetable plants

Space is key for healthy vegetables, so for plants that are direct-sown from seed, an essential step is to remove excess seedlings. This is known as thinning. It can be an emotional wrench sacrificing seedlings, but overcrowding the sprouted seedlings as they grow will stunt the plants and reduce your overall yield.

As the true leaves appear, remove seedlings and plant in a bigger space so the remaining plants are at the recommended spacing distances. If you are unable to remove the extras without disturbing the roots of the saved seedling, pinch the seedlings you wish to remove at the soil line. Keep the strongest, most robust seedlings.

Staking plants is a task that needs to be done early in the gardening season. Tall, climbing vegetables need staking or a trellis in place to climb up. It's important to stake after the plant has grown so that you don't damage the plant roots. However, the plants need to stake at planting time so they can grow upwards.

Later in the growing season, side shoots need to be pruned off the tomatoes. Pruning tomato side shoots means removing the growth that happens between the section where the stem and a branch collide. Tomato side shoots are shoots which appear in the joint between the stem and a branch of a tomato plant. When left unattended they become another main stem with branches, flowers, fruit, and even more side shoots. The tomato plant becomes unruly and burdened.

Pruning is recommended

Pruning tomato side shoots is in the best interest of the plant because the new stem competes for nutrients with the original plant. The tomato plant may have more fruit if you let the side shoots grow; however, the tomatoes will be smaller and the plant will be more unmanageable, requiring a lot of effort to stake as the summer progresses. Pruning tomato side shoots makes your tomato plants manageable and sturdy at the same time. There are other advantages. Pruning improves air flow and reduces the chances of disease, as fewer leaves dry faster if it rains or when watered. Pruning makes it more likely that pests will be spotted as they have fewer leaves to hide under. Pruning can also accelerate the ripening of the fruit.

Pruning is a good idea.

Weeds are ground hogs

Weeds are thieves. They steal food and water from your vegetables. At the beginning of the season it's always best to start with weed-free beds. Good weed management, such as removing them as soon as they appear, is the optimal approach to ensure they don't get out of control.

As well as keeping the soil around the beds clear of weeds, there is a lot of sense in also removing weeds from any surrounding lawn and pathways, because if they go to seed those weed seeds may infiltrate your vegetable patch. Ongoing weed management throughout the growing season will prevent any need for herbicides later in the summer.

Mulch is a gardener's friend

Surrounding your plants in mulch is one of the best things you can do. Mulches are loose coverings or sheets of material which are put onto the surface of soil. They can be applied to bare soil or to cover the surface of compost in pots. The purpose of mulch is to suppress weeds, cool the roots of the plant, and save water.

Seed-free straw is a good mulch for vegetable gardens. It offers a decent cover, is easy to clear aside for planting, and at the end of the season it can be turned into the soil. An added benefit is that pest-hungry spiders love to hide in straw and feast on garden critters.

Mulches can be split into two main groups: biodegradable and non-biodegradable. Both types suppress weeds by blocking sunlight which is needed to germinate and grow weed seeds, and conserve moisture by reducing evaporation from the soil surface.

Biodegradable mulches

The gradual breakdown of biodegradable mulch releases nutrients into the soil, which improves the soil structure. Once the materials have fully rotted down the layers will need replacing. Garden compost, wood chippings, straw (for strawberries), seaweed, well-rotted manure, spent hops (keep your dogs away as this is poisonous for them) and processed conifer bark all work well.

Non-biodegradable

Non-biodegradable mulches supress weeds and help retain moisture, but don't increase fertility or improve the soil structure. They can be a decorative addition, and slate, shingle, pebbles, gravel, stone chippings and other decorative aggregates can be used as mulch across beds. The darker the colour of the material the warmer the soil in the sun. Light coloured mulch such as white gravel reflects the sunlight and keeps the roots cooler in bright sunlight.

Mulch supresses weeds.

The best season to apply mulch
It is best to apply mulches from mid to late spring before the annual weeds geminate, and again in autumn, once the plants begin to die back. Apply them around the beds and plants. New plantings that require mulch to supress weed growth and retain moisture in the soil can be mulched at any time of the year.

Mulch application
Mulch the bed entirely, paying attention not to cover any low growing plants or to pile the mulch up too high against the stems of woody plants.

The thickness of biodegradable mulches should be between at least 5cm and ideally 7.5cm to be effective. Remove weeds and lay over moist soil, but make sure the soil is not frozen. Fruit trees need to be mulched to the edge of the canopy.

Cultivate the soil

Vegetables are hungry plants. It's important to nourish them with organic matter in the garden each year before planting and top up with more organic matter once or twice during the growing season. Different plants have different requirements; there is not a one size fits all solution so it's important to research the fertilising instructions required for the crops that are being planted.

The advantages of organic plant foods are that they are slow releasing. They continue to nourish your plants for the entire growing period. Should you choose a water-soluble fertiliser, it's important that prior to application your garden is well-watered.

Any investment in great soil in your vegetable garden is worth continuing for the entire growing season. A simple technique to protect and enrich your soil during the winter is to plant a crop of green manure in the autumn and then to transform it into the soil in the spring.

Green manures

Green manures are soil-covering, fast-growing plants. In vegetable gardens their foliage covers weeds while their roots stop soil erosion. They return valuable nutrients to the soil and improve soil structure while still green and dug into the ground.

Green manures improve soil structure.

When to sow

Sow green manures in late summer or autumn for the soil to soak up any nutrients, stopping the winter rain washing the nutrients away. During the following spring, they release these nutrients back into the soil when they are dug in. If you select a hardy green manure such as winter grazing rye and winter tares they will continue to grow throughout the winter before the spring, when they are integrated back into the soil.

Cover soil patches in the spaces between crops with green manures, or use green manures during intervals between crops. For example, rapid-growing mustard sown before mid-September can be integrated in October, or the frosted remains reused as mulch. Summer-grown green manures, for example buckwheat and fenugreek, cluster and create dense foliage which supresses weeds. In the summer, pea and bean family (legumes) green manures have greater capacity for storing the valuable plant nutrient nitrogen from the air to their roots. Green manures also offer protection of the soil surface from compaction by rain and provide shelter for garden friendly insects such as ground beetles.

Sowing green manures

Either sow the seeds in rows, or scatter them across the soil and then rake into the surface.

When you need the land to plant crops, cut the foliage down and then leave it to wilt. Turn over the plants and foliage into the top of the soil to 25cm.

Leave for roughly two weeks or more before sowing or planting out so the decaying green materials don't interfere with plant growth.

Green Manure Types

Perennial legumes

Alfalfa: Sow in April to July. Dig in after two or three months or leave for one to two years. Good for alkaline soils. Nitrogen releases only if the seed is inoculated with nitrogen-fixing bacteria before sowing.

Alsike clover: Sow in April to August. Dig in after two or three months or leave for one or two years; good for wet, acid soils.

Bitter blue lupin: Sow in March to June. Good for sandy, acid soils; leave for two or three months before digging in.

Crimson clover: Sow in March to August. Good for light soils. Leave in for two or three months up to flowering.

Essex red clover: Sow March to August. Overwinters well and can stay in for two or three months or for one or two years following sowing; good for loamy soils.

Annuals

Fenugreek: Only grows in the spring and summer. However, it is unlikely to create nitrogen in the UK.

Buckwheat: Sow in April to August. Can leave for two or three months after sowing; grows well on nutrient-depleted soils.

Grazing rye: Sow in August to November. Promotes soil structure and overwinters well. Turn over in the following spring.

Mustard: Sow in March to September and leave for two or three months before digging in. As it is a brassica, do not follow it by other brassicas, as this creates susceptibility to the disease clubroot.

CHAPTER 5
Harvesting the Fruits of your Labour

Timing is key when it comes to harvesting your vegetables. From the moment they are picked, the flavour, tenderness and nutritional value begin to diminish. Optimum picking is best when done as close as possible to eating. Every crop is different, so this is simply meant as a guide to steer you along the way and is by no mean definitive. The list of vegetables to grow is exhaustive, and could easily fill an almanac. So these pointers serve to indicate when a crop is ready to harvest.

Timing is key when harvesting.

But how do you know when they are ready?

Colour
Lots of vegetables change colours as they ripen, such as tomatoes and peppers. Make sure you read the seed packet, or research the colour so you know when they are ready to pick.

Glow
It is not unusual for ripe vegetables to have a shiny, sheen and healthy look when they are ready to be picked.

Size
Bigger is not always better. Generally speaking, vegetables are ready for harvest when they have grown to a useable size. To check the tenderness and flavour of a vegetable, taste a sample before picking to see if it is ready. Don't delay picking in order to grow bigger crops – the flavour could be reduced by over-growing.

Generally, vegetables can be harvested when they are around half-grown. This is when they have optimum tenderness and flavour. Crops which mature in late summer and early autumn are known to sometimes have a relatively lengthy harvest period which can be as long as two weeks or more. These crops can usually be stored for early winter use if you can't get them to the table right away. Wrap them in paper, and store in the dark and cool to prolong the storage time. If they are picked early season it's likely they will need to be eaten fresh. Some crops can be frozen or pickled if you are overrun.

Trial and error are part of the fun of growing your own food. With time your experience and taste will teach you when a crop is ready to be picked and eaten and when the flavour and tenderness are perfect.

Picking your crops can be very satisfying and rewarding.

Pick of the picks
Here are a select few top picking tips for a variety of vegetables to help you along the way.

Asparagus
When the stems reach 15cm to 25cm tall, less than 2.5cm diameter, and the bud tips are tight, asparagus are ready to pick. To pick them bend the stems until they snap. If the stem is too tough to snap is too tough to eat. At this stage pick all stems. Any stems that grow larger will negatively impact the plant's ability to send up new shoots. The crop harvest is completed when the stems no longer grow bigger than 1.5cm in diameter. Asparagus that is grown from crowns or seedlings needs time to become established and strong so needs two years in the ground before the first harvest.

Aubergine
Aubergine is ripe and ready to pick when the fruit is shiny, not dull, and around 7.5cm to 15cm long. If the sheen has dulled the fruit is overripe. After aubergine seeds have been sown it takes around 145 days to mature, and 70 days after seedlings have been planted. Immature fruits which are tender can still be eaten. The stems are tough so cut fruit from the plant with shears. To see if an aubergine has passed its peak, slice into it, and if the seeds are brown then it has gone over.

HARVESTING THE FRUITS OF YOUR LABOUR

Baby sweetcorn
Harvest the mini corn cobs when the silks at the end of the ears turn brown and damp and the ears are full and firm. The kernels need to be full, plump, and juicy and the peak of the husk should be round and blunt instead of pointed. Early varieties mature in about 75 days; late varieties can to take around 85 to 95 days. If you've planted the corn as late as midsummer it needs an extra 14 days to mature. To pick corn, take the cob and give it a sharp twist downwards to remove it from the stalk.

Runner beans
It's time to begin picking when the runner bean pods are 15–20cm long, and before the inner beans begin to swell.

It's important to pick regularly to stop any pods reaching maturity. At this point the plants will stop flowering and no more pods will be set. If you pick often the plants will continue to crop for around eight weeks and maybe more.

Dwarf and French beans
The beans are ready when they're 10cm long. You'll know they are ripe as they snap easily. If the beans can be seen through the pod they are past their prime. If picked often, dwarf French bean plants will continue to crop for a few weeks and climbing French beans even longer.

A basket of homegrown produce is delicious prize.

Beetroot
Pull beetroot when they are less than 5cm and not more than 7.5cm across, which is usually around eight to nine weeks following seed sowing. This the best time for beetroot as it will be most tender. If the beetroot remains in the ground too long it will be tough and woody. To check the size of the beetroot, move the soil away from the top of the planted root.

Broccoli
Broccoli is ready just before the flower buds open. Depending upon the variety this is around 14 to 60 weeks after sowing. Use a knife to harvest broccoli: cut the stem just beneath the top cluster of buds. Cropping here will stimulate the growth of more heads, which will be slightly smaller. Clusters of smaller buds will develop on side branches over the next 8 to 10 weeks. When yellow florets are visible broccoli is past harvest time.

Brussels sprouts
At about 16 weeks after sowing, when they are firm, pick the first sprouts. The Brussels will continue to be ready for picking throughout the following 6 weeks. Begin the harvest when the first sprouts are around 2.5cm to 5cm in diameter. Start at the bottom end of the stalk and work upwards as the sprouts grow. It's important to complete the harvest before the night temperatures drop below freezing. If it still has more crop to grow then dig up the plant and replant it in a site protected from the freezing temperatures, where the sprouts will continue to grow until the plant matures.

Cabbage
When the cabbage heads are formed and firm to touch, use a sharp knife to cut them at the base of the stalk. Early varieties tend to be ready around 105 to 115 days following sowing, whereas midseason varieties tend to be ready around 145 to 165 days. With the stalks left in place, there may be a second harvest from early varieties.

Carrots
Pull carrots up as soon as the roots are large enough to use. Keep harvesting as needed until the ground has begun to freeze.

Cauliflower
Cauliflowers are ready when the heads are compact and tight. Use a sharp knife to cut the stalk just below the head. White-budded varieties are ready for harvest 100 to 110 days after sowing whereas purple-budded varieties are ready 130 to 145 days from sowing. Varieties that need blanching could be ready a few days afterwards in warm weather. In cooler weather, heads can take up to two weeks to reach harvest after blanching. So, if possible, harvest early rather than late. If heads stay on the plant too long the curds begin to break apart into individual flowers. Blanching is the practice of tying large outer leaves together over and around developing cauliflower heads. This prevents them from yellowing or browning. If they absorb an abundance of sun exposure they can develop a bitter flavour. Some older white varieties can even turn shades of patchy purple

Celeriac
Harvest celeriac root crowns when they have grown to 5 to 10cm in diameter.

Celery
Celery can be eaten at all stages of growth and reaches maturity about 110 days after plants are set in the garden, which is around 180 days after sowing. When ready to harvest, cut individual stalks, or pull up the plant and cut the roots off beneath the base of the stalk. Work from the outside to the middle to harvest individual stalks.

Chard (Swiss)
Around 40 to 60 days after sowing seeds, with scissors or a sharp knife cut chard leaves when they are 15 to 25cm tall. Near the base of the plant, cut outer leaves with a sharp knife and the inner leaves will continue to grow. They can be cut a few days later. Remove old, wilted, or tough leaves so the plant produces new leaves.

Chicory
Leaf chicory heads can be cut from the roots when ready. Witloof chicory chicons can be harvested when about 15cm long by twisting the plant to break off the head.

Chinese leaves
At about 80 to 90 days after sowing seeds, all varieties of Chinese leaves (Chinese cabbage) are ready for harvest when the leaves are about 37cm long. Pull up the plant, cut off the roots and throw away tough outer leaves. Non-heading Chinese leaves can be harvested cut-and-come-again. Cut-and-come-again means to harvest the older outer leaves of leafy green vegetables. This enables the centre of the plant to continue sending out new leaves. It's an easy way to have a succession of harvests without having to remember to succession plant. Successional sowing is just sowing a row every few weeks. It also prevents the leaves from becoming bitter. Leave at least five leaves on the plant to promote a second harvest.

Cress
Cress grows quickly and is ready for harvest as soon as 10 days after the growth has started. Once the third leaf has appeared then garden cress is ready for harvest. Watercress is ready for harvest about 14 days after seed is sown. The tips of cress have the sweeter flavour.

Cucumber
Cucumbers are ready to be cut from the vine when they are 15cm to 18cm long and dark green and around 60 days after sowing. Pickling cucumbers can be cut from the vine when they are 3cm to 8cm long. Avoid leaving

Picking can be very satisfying.

the cucumber on the vine so long that it turns yellow or orange. Make sure that you pick cucumbers regularly or the plant will stop producing.

Endive, escarole
Endive and escarole reach maturity about 90 days after the seeds are sown. Pick endive and escarole leaves or plants at any size. The leafy heads can be cut off at the base of the leaves or leaves can be harvested cut-and-come-again. To blanch the leaves before harvest, bring the long outer leaves together over the crown of the plant and secure them together with an elastic band.

Fennel
The bulbous stem of fennel is ready for harvest when it measures between 7cm to 9cm in diameter. If the stem gets any larger it may be tough and stringy. Dig up the whole plant and cut off the roots and upper branches. The leaves of fennel can still be used to garnish and flavour when the plant is 50cm tall.

Garlic
Around 90 to 110 days after planting, garlic is ready for harvest when the tops begin to yellow and droop. As the leaves begin to yellow, stop watering and bend over the leaf tops so the bulb begins curing. Let the bulbs dry in a shady place for several days until the skin becomes papery. When they have completely dried then cut

off the leaf stalks and trim the roots. Young fresh garlic leaves taste like chives and can be trimmed to use as a herb to flavour dishes.

Globe artichoke

Globe artichokes need two years before they are ready for harvest in the second year after planting. Artichokes bud when plump but before the bracts open, and this is when they are ready to harvest. Pick the large central globe first and then pick the side-shoot globes. When the buds turn purple and the flowers become visible they are beyond harvest. Flower heads can be cut 12cm to 15cm down the stem.

Horseradish

Extract horseradish root after cool weather arrives in the autumn. Several frosts will enhance the flavour of horseradish. Use a hand fork to loosen the soil and lift the roots by hand. Horseradish needs around 120 days to reach maturity.

Jerusalem artichoke

In autumn or early winter, after the foliage has died back, lift the tubers. Loosen the soil with a garden fork then pull the tuber from the ground. Jerusalem artichokes require about 120 days to mature.

Leeks

About 16 to 18 weeks after sowing, leeks are ready for harvest when stems are 5cm in diameter. At full maturity leek stems will be around 8cm around. Pull the leeks out by hand or dig out with a garden fork.

Lettuce
Some 10 to 11 weeks after sowing, iceberg, cos and butterhead lettuce are ready for picking. Use a sharp knife to cut off the whole head at the root crown. Using sharp scissors, snip loose-leaf lettuce leaf by leaf, cutting outer leaves when they are large enough to use. This is around 6 to 7 weeks after sowing. At about 11 to 12 weeks after sowing, romaine lettuce will be ready for harvest. All lettuce leaves are edible at any stage of growth.

Mustard
Mustard leaves should be picked cut-and-come-again when leaves are 20cm to 25cm long, or the entire plant can be harvested. This is when the flavour is best. Older leaves can be cooked. Depending on the variety mustard takes around 30 to 50 days to reach maturity after sowing.

Onion
Dependent upon variety, bulb onions are ready for pulling about 3 to 5 months after the seeds are sown, or around 3.5 months after sets, or young plants, have been set out. Keep an eye out for when leaves begin to yellow and the stems bend to a nearly horizontal position, which stops the growth of the bulb and it begins to ripen. Get rid of the soil from around the top half of the bulb. When the leaves turn brown, pull the bulbs. Bunching, or green onions or scallions, can be harvested young when needed from a few weeks after sowing. Scallions have the best flavour when pulled less than 25cm long.

Parsnip
Parsnips planted in the spring are ready for pulling in early autumn, around four months after seeds are sown. The flavour of parsnip roots can be improved by waiting until a few hard frosts have passed. Leaving them in the ground all winter will make them full of flavour. Pull the parsnips left in the ground over the winter before new growth starts again in spring.

Pea
Pick green pea pods when the pods are firm but still plump. Don't let them begin to yellow or to shrivel. Green peas are usually ready for picking about three weeks after flowering, or between 60 to 70 days after sowing. Mangetout, and other edible-pod peas should be picked when the pods are flat and the peas inside are tiny. Snip pea pods from the plant with scissors, or pruners, rather than pulling them off the vine. It's ok to leave garden peas on the vine to wither and turn brown, then to pick, shell, dry them out and store as dried peas.

Peas (Sugar snap)
Pick sugar snap peas when they are still crunchy enough to be able to snap them in half and before the seeds fill out the pods. This is when the pods are tender, moist, and succulent. Time from sowing to picking varies depending on variety, and is normally between 8 and 9 weeks.

Pepper
Sweet peppers and chilli peppers can be eaten at any stage of growth – including immature or full size, or green or red. After 60 to 20 days peppers reach maturity once they have been planted. Chilli peppers can be picked fully ripe for drying or pickling. Snip the fruit from the plant with scissors rather than pull.

Potato
Young potatoes or new potatoes can be pulled as soon as 45 to 55 days after planting, around the time the blossoms appear, or a few weeks later. Pull new potatoes as soon as they reach a useable size. Early varieties of

Fresh produce is delicious.

potatoes are the best for new potatoes. Late varieties should be pulled around the arrival of the first autumn frost and can continue to harvest for two to three weeks once the tops have died back. Pull up the large tubers which gives the smaller potatoes time to grow. It's best to dig up potatoes in dry weather and handle carefully so the potatoes don't bruise.

Pumpkin

Four months after sowing pick pumpkins when the leaves die, the hue of the fruit is a rich orange and the sheen of the skin has faded. Cut pumpkins from the vine at full maturity just before the first autumn frost. Use pruning shears, leaving about 7cm to 8cm of stem on the fruit; pumpkins decay quickly if the stems are broken rather than cut. After harvesting, set pumpkins in the sun for one to two weeks to harden the outer skin, then store them in a cool dry place.

Radish

Around 25 to 30 days after sowing, early and mid-season radishes are ready for pulling. Later varieties take around 60 days. They are ready when the roots reach the size listed for each variety, usually less then 2cm in diameter or as soon as they large enough to eat. Make sure that you don't leave it so late that the radishes become tough and woody.

Raspberries

The early summer raspberries are ready for picking in early summer, and autumn raspberries don't mature until later in the summer. Pick on a dry day.

GROW YOUR OWN FOOD

Sweet, succulent and ready for eating.

Redcurrants
It is worth noting that in a good year redcurrant can crop so heavily that the branches might bow or break. If so, support the branches by tying them to stakes or canes. When the berries are well coloured, shiny, and taste sweet they are ready for picking. If they are dull it's too late. They won't all ripen at exactly the same time so you can pick them over two or three times. It's best to pick the whole strig (cluster of berries) at the same time instead of individual fruit.

Rhubarb
As rhubarb is a perennial, it takes two years to be ready after planting. Harvest leafstalks that are 25cm to 40cm long and 2.5cm or more in diameter. Cut the stalks before they become tough. Let the smaller stalks continue to grow to build the plant's strength. Cut each stalk near the base and follow by a sideward twisting tug. The stalk should separate cleanly from the top of the roots. You can cut rhubarb for up to eight to ten weeks.

Shallots
You can pull shallots at any stage of growth to use as green onions. For dry bulbs, pull shallots when the tops have browned and withered, which is around 100 days after sowing.

Sorrel
Sorrel is ready about 70 days after sowing. The sorrel leaves can be cut at any time during the growing season. Young and tender leaves taste the best. Cut outer leaves as needed cut-and-come-again.

Spinach

Pick about six weeks after planting when they are 15cm to 20cm long. To keep the picking plentiful and extend the harvest, cut leaves cut-and-come-again, starting with outer leaves and allowing inner leaves to keep re-growing. Pick continuously until the seed stalk appears or until the weather turns very cold. Then cut back individual leaves or the entire plant at the soil surface.

Squash (Summer)

Around 50 days after sowing, summer squash is ready for picking when the fruits are tender and easily punctured. Pick summer squash when the skin yields to thumb pressure. Courgette is best when about 17cm long and 3cm thick. Patty pan summer squash is ready for picking when the fruit is 5cm in diameter. Patty pan is tastiest when about 8cm across. Straight neck squash is best when about 10cm long. For the tastiest flavour, harvest summer squash at no more than 15cm to 20cm long.

Squash (Winter)

Winter squash is ready for cutting when the skin is extremely hard, usually around 80 to 115 days after planting, variety dependent. It's best to delay the harvest of winter squash until just before the first hard frost. A few light frosts changes starch to sugar and amplifies the flavour. Cut winter squash from the vine but leave a 5cm to 7cm stem on it. If you can leave winter squash to cure in the sun for a week or two, then store in a cool, dry place over the winter to use when needed.

Strawberries

It's best to pick strawberries when they are bright red all over. It is best to do this during the warmest part of the day as this is when they taste the best. Try to eat them as fresh as possible as they don't keep for long once they are ripe.

Homegrown summer fruits are the best.

Sweet potato

Sweet potatoes are ready around 90 days after planting. Dig them up as soon as the first autumn frost hits the tops of the plants. Don't leave them in the ground after the first frost as dying vines can spread rot into the tubers. You can pull them earlier in the season, but they grow to their optimum size in the last 30 days of growth. You have to dig up sweet potatoes carefully with a spade or fork as they bruise easily and this can cause decay if storing them. Dry sweet potatoes for two or three hours after pulling them up. Spread them out on paper and dry in a place warm place with a consistent temperature of 26°C for 10 days to two weeks. Gradually reduce the temperature to 10° by ventilating the curing place.

Swede

Swede are ready for harvest around 90 days after seed sowing. Select swede about 8cm to 15cm long, but not longer than 15cm to 17cm. Swede tastes best after the first autumn frost but before the roots freeze. Grab the top of the swede and pull it up.

Tomato

Tomatoes can be harvested when they are in full colour. Pick the tomato by gently lifting each tomato until the stem snaps. Tomatoes do not develop their natural red colour in temperatures greater than 30°C; in hot regions, pick tomatoes when they are still pink and allow them to ripen fully indoors. You can also pick green tomatoes and let them ripen indoors if the temperatures aren't warm enough.

Turnip

Around 40 days after sowing turnips are ready for pulling up, when roots are 5 cm in diameter. Don't let turnip roots grow larger than 7cm or they become woody and lose flavour. To pick them grab the top of the turnip and pull it up.

CHAPTER 6

Foraging

Foraging for food is an ancient art, born of a slow and elegant past of feeding and sustaining ourselves from the land. The benefits reach far beyond simply putting food on the table. The very act of foraging for wild edible plants can be transformative and rewarding.

For some, collecting and eating the riches of the woodlands and hedgerows has been part of life since childhood. For others, gathering wild food is a new experience. Hedgerows and woodlands can be great places to forage for free food. There is a range of edible species ready to be transformed into jams, gins and more.

The legality of foraging is reasonably simple – if the item is being grown as a crop, then it's not foraging, it's scrumping (or stealing!). It's highly unlikely that cob nuts or blackberries growing in a field hedge are intended as a food crop; however, the nuts and sloes in a person's garden hedge will be! Therefore, if someone's caring for a tree or a hedge, or if it's in an orchard or garden or looks intentionally planted, tread with care! That said, there are lots of edible crops grown incidentally on trees planted ornamentally, on streets and in council amenity spaces, particularly in urban areas – foraging doesn't have to be just a country pursuit! Look out for apples, plums and cherries, too!

Wild garlic

As it grows in shady and damp conditions, the wild garlic season starts in late winter and lasts until the end of spring. It's so exciting when it arrives because it means it is time to go foraging for this delicious herb, which you can make into a tasty soup, pesto or simply blend it with olive oil and salt and store in a jar. Then add it liberally to mayonnaise with some freshly squeezed lime juice.

The unmistakable scent in woodlands and forests is the fresh, garlicky smell of wild garlic. Wild garlic has a lighter, fresher flavour to traditional bulb garlic, and the green, pointed leaves and white flowers of this bulbous perennial flowering plant make it easily identifiable.

Wild garlic grows in dense clumps, covering woodland floors at its peak. The deep green leaves are long and pointed with a smooth edge, and are best picked young. Wild garlic flowers are delicate white clusters and bloom in mid spring. These edible flowers can be added to salads and other dishes.

Early autumn is peak foraging. It's when hedgerows and trees are laden with the jewel-like colours of ripening fruits and nuts from August onwards.

Wild garlic is nature's gift.

Blackberry

Blackberrying is probably the one traditional foraging activity that's still widely enjoyed today. Picking blackberries, the fruit of bramble, is a pastime enjoyed across the generations and is a great family pursuit.

Blackberries have a high Vitamin C content and can be eaten raw or cooked. There are hundreds of micro species with subtly different flavours. Great to bake with blackberry loaf, crumble or pie. Add to vodka with sugar and rest until Christmas or simply jam or compote.

Seek out: this unmistakable, prickly shrub grows in woods, hedges, heathland and wasteland almost everywhere. Pick the berries when they're a deep purple-black from late July and throughout autumn.

Rosehip

Commonly found in hedgerows, rose hips are the red and orange seed pods of rose plants.

The hips have a fleshy covering that contains the hairy seeds (the irritant hairs were traditionally used by schoolboys to make itching powder). The outside is packed with Vitamin C and they are well known for helping stave off winter colds. They are good for jellies and jams, and can be used to make a lightly infused rosehip syrup for cordial or for pouring onto ice cream or pancakes.

Seek out: look for bright red rosehips from September to November along hedgerows and woodland edges. Cut, or carefully pull, the hips close to the base of each pod (to avoid being attacked by prickly thorns).

Sloes

The blackthorn is best known for its crop of tart, acidic fruits used to make the deep-red, wintry drink, sloe gin.

The general rule is to pick after the first frost as it softens the skins and helps to release the juices. However, you can pick them early and freeze at home instead and prick them with a pin, or if you are like me, put them in a freezer bag and whack them with a rolling pin. Make sloe gin or try using sloes for whisky, jams and vinegar.

Seek out: the blue-black berries are ready for picking from the end of September to December. In some years, blackthorn trees along hedgerows and fields are heavy with fruit.

Bullace

On a good year, bullace fruits can literally weigh down the hedgerow.

The fruits are similar to the small damson, and like the damson are a type of plum and can be used to make crumbles, jams and preserves, fruit wine and to make fruit liqueurs (like sloe gin).

Seek out: small, oval fruits can vary in colour but are usually blue, purple or black. They tend to taste acidic until they're ripe. This is a great late season fruit as it ripens up to six weeks later than many others, from October to November.

Hazelnut

A common tree in woods, hedgerows and gardens, it bears its crop of nuts (also called cobnuts and filberts) from late August.

You gather the hazelnuts early in the season, when they're still green, and the shelled nuts make a tasty nibble to munch on while you're out walking. If you collect enough, the shelled nuts can be roasted in the oven or used to make hazelnut butter.

Seek out: it's advisable to collect hazelnuts when they're still young and green in late August to mid-September. Most ripe nuts are found in September and October, depending on the weather.

Sweet chestnut

Popular pickings, and a Christmas classic, sweet chestnut trees are not native to the UK but were introduced by the Romans.

The nuts can be baked, roasted, boiled or microwaved. Don't forget to score a cross in them to stop them from exploding. Once cooked and peeled they can be eaten as they are or used in desserts and stuffing. You can also candy them, puree them or store them in syrup.

Seek out: you'll find the best crop at the foot of large established trees. Trees start dropping nuts from October and into late autumn and early winter.

Walnut

Walnut trees, like the sweet chestnut, were also first introduced to the UK by the Romans.

Crack open the shells to get to the nut. Watch out though, because there is a reason Walnuts are used to stain furniture. When peeling them, gloves are advised unless you want to look like your hands have experienced a fake tan disaster. They can be eaten raw (when they're 'wet'), dried or pickled. Dried nuts can be stored for around a year. They can be added to both sweet and savoury dishes. Add spinach, garlic, extra virgin olive oil and blend dried walnuts to make a great pesto. Season with crunchy Himalayan salt.

Seek out: trees can be found throughout the UK, often in large gardens and parks. The nuts are covered with a green, fleshy husk that starts to split as it ripens. Pick them in late autumn and early winter.

Walnuts are versatile and tasty.

CHAPTER 7

Keeping Chickens

Chickens are so much fun.

I can really only touch upon the basics of keeping chickens. As you can imagine there are entire books written about keeping chickens, and a plethora of different breeds. My aim is to give you an overview so you can get started with the basic requirements to care for your chickens safely and healthily.

Keeping chickens

Chickens are so much fun to keep. They bring a great energy to the garden. If you have children they are wonderful animals to look after and very hands-on for children all ages. (Although cockerels can be feisty so may not be suitable to keep around small children.) Let's not forget the delight of a ready supply of fresh eggs.

Please bear in mind that it is an offence to be cruel to any captive or domestic animal by anything that you do or have omitted to do.

Code of recommendations for the welfare of laying hens

Defined by DEFRA (Department for Environment, Food and Rural Affairs). This code says hens should have five freedoms:

1. Freedom from hunger and thirst by ready access to fresh water and a diet to maintain full health and vigour.
2. Freedom from discomfort by providing an appropriate environment, including shelter and a comfortable resting area.
3. Freedom from pain, injury or disease by prevention and rapid diagnosis and treatment.
4. Freedom to express natural behaviour by providing space, sufficient facilities and the company of the animal's own kind.
5. Freedom from fear and distress by ensuring conditions and treatment to avoid mental suffering.

Chickens make great pets.

A poultry pact – chickens

Chickens need daily care, just like any other pet. You can't abandon them for a week's holiday without organising someone to come and care for your chickens while you are away. But don't worry because they are easy to care for and not too much effort for your chicken minder, who I'm sure would be easily appeased with the rewards of some delicious fresh eggs.

It's worth noting that existing pets may also have to share their lives – and garden – with your chickens. If you have cats or dogs, free-range hens can be a temptation. Depending on the breed and nature of your pets they will probably get used to each other, but if not, you will then need to provide a sturdy chicken coop and run space to keep chickens in, and your larger furry animals out.

Is it legal to keep chickens in my garden?

Over 700,000 people in the UK already keep chickens in their gardens, and generally speaking, if you are keeping a few hens for eggs then there shouldn't be any problems. To be certain, it's important to examine the deeds or any lease for your home to make sure they don't expressly forbid the keeping of livestock and chickens. It's worth checking with your local council which may have by-laws concerning chickens. For peace of mind it's important to make sure that you are allowed to keep chickens on your premises.

Clucking decibels

Are you worried that your feathered friends are going to be noisy? Generally, they are quite self-contained with a gentle clucking. They sometimes make a few loud squawks and clucks to proudly announce they have just laid an egg. If you decide to keep a cockerel then they are noisy birds and can start crowing from 4am onwards and like to exercise their vocal chords all day. You don't need to keep a cockerel for your chickens to lay unless you are planning to let your chickens sit on their eggs and hatch out chicks. But be warned, if you do this you may end up with even more noisy cockerels.

How much time do you have?

Chickens usually need to be checked on twice a day. Obviously, you can create a contained area with automated self-feeding equipment and a ready supply of water and then leave them unattended, but they still need regular checks. My personal preference is to check on them in the morning and in the evening. I tend to collect the eggs and feed them in the morning and then again check on them again in the evening to make sure they have gone to bed.

So how many chickens should you start with?

If you are just starting out it's probably best to start with two or three birds to see how you get on. Chickens like to live in groups so never keep less than a pair. This is where expressions such as, pecking order and head of the hen house are derived. Even a small group of chickens has an established chicken hierarchy, which they work out themselves. Chickens do need natural light and sunshine to lay properly, and often slow down, or even stop, in the winter months; but three chickens should provide enough eggs to feed a family of four.

Eggxactly how many eggs can you expect?

According to the International Egg Commission, the UK average egg consumption per person is approximately 180 eggs a year, or just under 3.5 eggs a week. On this basis a family of four would eat about 12 to 14 eggs a week, and it would be reasonable to eggspect this number of eggs from 2 to 3 chickens. Different breeds of chicken lay different numbers of eggs.

KEEPING CHICKENS

Your own fresh eggs taste better than ones bought in a shop.

For example, a Light Sussex may lay up to 220 eggs a year, while a showier breed such as the Orpington may only produce 80 eggs a year. A good starter is to rehome hybrid chickens which have been living in battery conditions and have slowed their lay rate down and so are due to be culled. The internet or social media are good places to look for ex-battery hens to rehome and you can sometimes save them for free or as a little as £3 per hen. They are good layers and often arrive in a scraggy condition. It's heart-warming to watch them fluff up and enjoy a happy life in their new home.

Egg production also decreases when a hen moults, which can happen at any time but usually occurs at the end of summer. As hens get older, their egg production can also slow down.

Housing your hens

Before you rush out and get hens you need to decide where and how you are going to house them. This will most likely be your biggest outlay of cash so you will want to get it right. With so many chicken coop suppliers both on and offline it can feel a bit overwhelming when you first start out. Hopefully, after this section of the guide, you will know what to look for in a chicken coop and what to avoid.

The purpose of a chicken coop

The purpose of a chicken coop is to provide sanctuary for your hens to lay their eggs and a safe and secure place to roost at night. Usually, they do this in the coop – lay eggs and rest safely at night.

Chickens love to roam and scratch.

Chickens are natural foragers, and from dawn until dusk they will want to be out and about scratching around for food, so it's important that they have access to a decent sized, well drained, area for them to scratch about in. You can have them roaming free range on your garden and they are excellent weeders but unfortunately as scavengers they don't discern between weed and plant. If your garden is wild and unkempt then free roaming chickens are a great addition, but if it's manicured and neat I would think carefully about releasing them. You will also need to keep them away from your veggie patch as they will feast away on all your plants.

If free range is not your solution then this problem can be solved with a chicken coop and extendable run, which only take up a few metres of space and can be moved around the garden. The other option is to create a dedicated chicken area.

Getting cooped up

There are 7 key questions to consider when deciding upon which chicken coop to choose:

1. Is it big enough for the number of birds you wish to keep?

There are guidelines on the minimum space per bird, which according to DEFRA is 1 sq. foot (0.09m^2) per bird.

KEEPING CHICKENS

The UK Poultry Club (founded in 1877) recommends at least 1 sq. foot (0.09m^2) per bird (large fowl) or 8in (20cm) square for bantams.

This is the minimum and the more room the birds have the better for the quality of life and the better their temperament. It it's too cramped they can get agitated as they don't enjoy being 'cooped up' in cramped conditions. The more space you give them the happier they will be. Cramped conditions lead to boredom, pecking and an increased likelihood of pests and diseases.

However, if you let your hens free-range during the day and you only lock them up in their house at night then it will be OK if there is less space than the DEFRA recommendations. The hens will perch tightly together at night, although too many hens in a coop could result in health problems, not to mention a lot more cleaning.

When working out the size of chicken coop required, whether online or in a shop, check the internal measurements of the sleeping/roosting area of the coop are in square feet and remember to allow at least 1 sq. foot (0.09m^2) per bird.

If your plan is to keep your chickens in a coop with a run for most of the time, try and allow around 1 square meter of run space for each bird. If the run is situated on the grass, expect the grass to wear thin and turn in to a bit of a quagmire when it rains. Some people prefer to keep their coop and run on a hard standing. This has the advantage of there being a little less mud about when it rains; it can be sprayed down and cleaned regularly with a hose or high pressure cleaner and there is also less chance of a determined fox tunnelling in under the run.

But it does create a bit of an unnatural environment for them so it is worth giving your hens a really good layer of bark to allow them to behave naturally and scratch about in. They will also need access to a dry area of soil for them to take regular dust baths. Hens will need and want to take a regular dust bath to rid their feathers of parasites and insects.

If they don't have access to an area of dry soil then you should provide them with some. This can be done by filling a deep tray or a large low flat with soil and sand. If allowed to free range they usually identify a secluded spot in the garden to dig their dust bath.

Free-range birds have plenty to keep them occupied but hens housed permanently in a run may need things to keep them entertained. They enjoy different levels of height to jump onto and perch on, and some chicken owners hang CDs in the run which give them something to peck at. You can give also them a ready supply of leafy greens for them to eat.

A poultry electric netting kit to provide a safe and secure area for you hens to roam is also an option but you will need to consider if you have space and budget (£150 to £200) for one of these.

If you do decide to fence off a dedicated area for your chickens then you must factor in foxes. Make sure foxes can't access their run by simply climbing over or tunnelling under. Foxes are savage predators and will kill all your chickens even if they only take one to eat. I have lost my entire flock of birds to a fox attack and it is not a welcome sight to behold. More on Mr Fox later...

2. The convenience of cleaning and egg collection

Egg collection is usually a daily occurrence, so choose a chicken coop that gives easy access to those eggs, with the minimum disturbance to your hens. Make sure that the house is situated so that you can lift the lid on the nesting boxes, grab and go.

To ensure that your hens remain in good health, regular cleaning of the hen house is required. The longer it is the left the worse it gets, and neglecting your chickens can make them susceptible to mite infestations and other pests, which are much more hassle to deal with than regularly cleaning out the coop.

So, when selecting a chicken coop the ease of cleaning should be a major consideration. Look for hen houses which have easy access to the nesting area as well as pull out trays and removable perches. Regular cleaning will not only avoid the build-up of droppings but also reduces the opportunities for pests and diseases to take hold. A weekly clean should only take around 15 minutes in a well-made and maintained hen house.

3. Is your coop well ventilated?
A chicken coop can quickly become toxic due the high level of ammonia released by the chicken's droppings. Inadequate ventilation can lead to respiratory problems in your birds, so it is important to ensure that fresh air circulates. However, chickens do not cope well with draughts so there is a balance to be achieved, and the ventilation must be such that there are no draughts. Ventilation can be achieved with ventilation holes or sliding doors in the side of the coop. If you make sure the ventilation holes are near the top of the coop it allows for the toxic air to escape without your chickens being caught in any draughts.

4. Hen safety and security
It's important to secure your coop against predators, including foxes and also egg-stealing rats. Raising your coop off the ground offers better protection from predators trying to dig their way in. Check your coop and run when collecting any eggs for any signs of damage or gnawing, as these are a sign of potential predators trying to get in.

Make sure your hen house is weatherproofed sufficiently for the weather it will endure, and if you choose a wooden coop then consider treating it with animal-friendly preservatives, ideally once a year, to protect it from the elements.

If you have chickens, there will most likely be foxes. Urban foxes are as prevalent as their country cousins, and are a major consideration for any chicken owner.

Your chicken coop and run must be both secure and robust enough to resist a determined attack by a fox. Foxes kill chickens without discrimination so even if they take one to eat they will kill the whole peep. Foxes will attack at any time night or day. The best defence is to make sure your hens are safe and sound in a sturdy, robust hen house.

They are also highly effective diggers and can easily tunnel under a coop wall and into the run, so the smart solution is to lock your hens up at night inside the actual housing area of the coop.

A layer of bricks or pavers around your run will help prevent digging foxes. Always inspect your chicken coop for signs of scratching or teeth marks, and repair quickly any holes to prevent them from becoming larger.

Keeping chickens can attract vermin with any leftover food. Rats are most likely to come and visit the chicken coop during the winter, when other food is scarce. Rats rarely attack chickens as such, but they will steal their eggs. Rats are opportunists who love a free meal, so the best way to discourage rats is to keep your chicken coop clean and free from surplus food.

Mice and small vermin are less of a problem because chickens are omnivores and will eat them if they get too close. If your cat catches a mouse and leaves it as a dead gift, chuck it in to the chickens and they will eat it up.

Make sure that your chicken feed is securely stored away. Simply putting it up high on a shelf won't discourage mice or rats: you need to keep your feed in a container with a secure lid, such as a large galvanised dustbin. I had my chicken feed in a plastic dustbin with a lid and the rats gnawed a hole into the lid to eat it.

5. Perfect perches
Roosting hens like to perch as high above the ground as they can, to give them a sense of safety from predators. Perches made from plastic or metal piping are not suitable for chickens, as they cannot grip the perch properly.

Chickens prefer to perch on a flat surface with gently curving edges so their feet are protected as they grip onto it. The perch should be about 3 to 4 cm wide, with curved edges. Makes sure the perches in your coop are wooden wide, flat and rounded off along the top edges.

It's important that you are able to remove your perches for cleaning, and they need to be positioned well away from food or water. A chicken can create over 50% of their droppings during the night.

6. Nesting boxes

Hens will always seek out dark, quiet and secluded places to lay their eggs. By creating suitable nesting boxes in the coop, your hens have ideal laying spaces for their eggs which will be clean, protected and easily accessible.

A hen house with the nesting box protruding from the side with access via a nesting box lid means you can easily collect eggs. Hens like to cosy up with each other, so don't be surprised if you find two or even more birds huddled together in a single nesting box, leaving any others vacant.

Line your nesting boxes with soft dry bedding material and make sure they are slightly lower than the perches, otherwise the occupants will poop in the boxes and sit in it all night. So, to keep your eggs clean make sure your perches are higher than the nesting boxes.

7. Coop appeal and endurance

Your chicken coop will be part of your garden 365 days a year, so it should be something you are happy to look at, and not be an eyesore. But more importantly, will it last? There are plenty of chicken coops for sale for under £200 and while they may appear great value for money, are they robust enough to protect your chickens and endure the weather of the seasons? Budget is obviously a key factor in your decision and it is worth trawling the internet for pre-loved ones if new is beyond your reach. Key things to consider are size and durability – can it withstand the weather and the gnawing teeth of greedy predators?

Chickens are reasonably low maintenance.

A day in the life of a chicken keeper

On the whole, chickens are reasonably low maintenance pets, which just get on with their own existence. Typically, you will need to let your hens out first thing every morning, and either fill their feeder with feed or scatter their feed on the ground and fill their water dispensers with fresh, clean water.

Chickens will usually lay in the morning. They will come out to eat and then disappear back into the coop to lay an egg. Ideally, you should check and remove any eggs from the nesting boxes as soon as they have laid. This is to prevent accidental damage or one of your hens actually eating the egg. It also lessens the chances of the egg getting muck on it, although if they do I give mine a quick rinse in cold water to clean them. Chickens produce waste as and where they need, which can be in the nesting box too.

However, if you work and only get back in the evening to collect their eggs, that is also fine. Your chickens will happily scratch about until dusk, when you should return to collect any new eggs. Make a quick check for any wet or soiled bedding, which should be removed, and then shut your hens away, safe from predators.

Your chicken coop should be cleaned once a week, or twice a month if you only have a few hens. However, it is worth doing a 'poo pick' in the morning, which just involves carefully scooping up the poop in the hen house and throwing it on the compost heap. Chickens produce a surprisingly large amount of waste during both the day and night.

Feeding your hens

Your chickens can obtain up to 25% of their protein by foraging for grass and insects.

Your hens, however, should always be fed a complete chicken food of either pellets or meal to keep them in top laying condition. The average hen will eat between 100–150 grams of complete food a day. With 3 hens expect to use a 20kg bag of layers pellets every 40 to 50 days. Chicken feed can be bought online or from local farmers, a feed supply store, or even high street pet stores.

Chickens need lots of fresh water.

Even if you use layers pellets this can also be supplemented with around 20 grams of grain or corn per bird per day.

But a little tip is to NOT feed them grain and chicken feed mixed together or in the morning. The chickens will simply pick out the tasty grain, filling their crops and reducing their intake of the more nutritious complete food, or like my current birds just eat the layers pellets and leave the corn. However, an unbalanced diet can adversely affect egg production, so grain should be given as a treat, perhaps in the afternoon when the day's supply of fresh shoots and pellets has been eaten.

In days of yore it was common to feed chickens leftover kitchen scraps. However, it is actually illegal to feed catering waste, kitchen scraps, meat or meat products to farmed animals, and this would also likely apply to a few chickens kept in the back garden.

This is to prevent the introduction and spread of potentially devastating notifiable animal diseases, such as African and Classical Swine Fever, and Foot and Mouth disease. So, although it is tempting to toss your left over pasta or rice to your chickens, you are technically breaking the law.

Water is the elixir of life

Fresh water is critical to the health and survival of your chickens. An egg is made up of 65% water – so you must give your chickens access to fresh water. Chickens have little regard for keeping their water clean and fresh. They kick dirt into and even poo in it so it is important to keep the water fresh daily if possible.

Once the water is dirty, they tend not to drink from it, so a solution is to raise the water dish or feeder above ground level and place it near to the entrance to the coop, so they can easily access it.

Other solutions include hanging the drinker and feeder from something so it is at your hens' shoulder height. However, even if you do this the water will still get dirty. When they drink, their beaks get wet. They then peck at something in the soil, go back and have a few more sips to wash whatever it was they managed to get, and in the process, deposit the soil that stuck to their beak.

It could be worth investing in a few plastic gravity feed drinkers which should be scattered about the garden or run area, so there is always the option of a clean source of water. I have a big trough that I rinse and refill regularly which ensures a substantial water supply.

Water is critical to the health of your hens and it is worth noting that on a hot day a single hen can drink as much as half a litre so make sure you keep an eye on their supply when the sun is out.

Gritty business

As hens don't have teeth (cue phrase, rare as hen's teeth), they ingest grit into their gizzards, where it helps break up their food. If your chickens don't have access to natural grit in the ground, you should provide some. Grit, with added oyster shell, has the benefit of a higher calcium content which helps create stronger egg shells. Keep your grit handy and you can mix it in with the feed. The hens will peck at it as and when they need it.

A bit about bedding

Wood shavings, chopped straw and shredded paper can all be used as chicken bedding.

Wood shavings are popular as they are cheap and help to reduce the ammonia smell. They provide a soft surface and insulate the hen house well.

Aim for a reasonable quality bedding and it should dry quickly too, as wet bedding is a haven for parasites, mould and bacteria, none of which will do your chickens any good.

Spread the bedding on the floor of the chicken coop to absorb moisture, droppings and smells. This layer also acts as a soft surface for the hens' feet and as insulation in the winter.

Bedding should also be placed in the nesting boxes to protect the eggs and to provide more comfort for the hens. I also like to include a mix of hay and straw on top of the shavings for the hens to nest in.

However, make sure if you decide to use wood shavings as your choice of bedding that they are 'dust free' or 'dust extracted', otherwise they can cause respiratory problems for your hens. Shredded paper is the cheapest option if you own a shredder and have access to plenty of paper. But it does get soiled very quickly and you will need to change it more frequently.

Hemp which has been cut up and dried is also good for lining the nest box.

Coop cleaning

This is fairly self-explanatory but to clean out the coop, clear out the shavings and any straw. The flush the coop with a hose, or if you are feeling ambitious use a pressure hose as long as your coop is robust enough. Take out the perches and give them a scrub down – hose or pressure wash if necessary. Once washed give it an airing for an hour to dry it out then add in new fresh bedding. Add fouled bedding to your compost heap or throw away.

Index

Alfalfa, 89
alliums, 38, 75
aggregate fruit, 43
annuals, 90
aphids, 54, 59, 70–1, 80
apples, 43, 63, 66, 78, 104
apricots, 58
artichokes, 32, 42, 48–50, 52, 54, 56, 58, 65, 98
    see also, Jerusalem artichoke
asparagus, 32, 39, 47–8, 50, 52, 54, 56, 58, 64, 93
aubergines, 7, 41, 45–6, 48–50, 52, 54, 56–7, 80, 94

bacterial infection, 34
bacterial wilt disease, 80
basil, 52, 63, 64
    sweet basil, 47, 49, 51, 53, 55, 57
bean:
    legumes, 15, 44, 89
    propagation, 32
    soy, French, 42, 57, 94
    broad, 45–53, 55, 57–9, 63–5, 67
    sprouts, dwarf, runner, 50, 52, 54, 56, 58, 60, 63, 94
bedding, 116–19
beetroot, 37, 48–53, 55, 57, 59, 62, 64, 95
berry, 43
birds, 27, 54, 56, 58, 63, 73, 80, 83, 111, 113–16, 118
blackberries, 43, 56, 58, 63–4, 68, 104, 106
blackcurrants, 35, 68
blackfly, 59
blight, 60–1
blueberries, 43
brassicas, 71, 74, 90
broccoli, 32, 42, 48, 50–4, 56, 58, 62, 64, 66, 72, 74, 95
Brussel sprouts, 47, 49–50, 52–6, 58–9, 95
budding, 32, 37

bulbs, 38, 66, 98–9, 102
bullace, 107

cabbage, 32, 40, 46–9, 51, 53, 55–60, 63–5, 95
cabbage white butterfly, 71–2
cabbage root fly, 74
capsules, 44
carrots, 7, 38, 45, 47, 50–1, 55–6, 64, 73, 95
Carrot root fly, 55–6, 73
caterpillars, 71–2, 74, 79
cauliflower, 32, 42, 45–7, 49, 51, 53–5, 57, 64, 72, 74, 96
celeriac, 50, 52, 54, 56, 58, 73, 96
celery, 32, 39, 47–8, 50, 55, 63, 73, 96
chard, 59, 66, 96, 104
cherries, 58, 104
chickens, 83, 109, 111–18
chicory, 58, 68, 96
chillies, 47, 63
Chinese cabbage leaves, 59–60, 96
chives, 7, 50, 52, 54, 56, 58, 65, 98
cloches, 52–4, 57, 65, 67
clover, 90
codling moth, 78
cold frames, 48, 50, 54, 66
compost, 7, 14–15, 17, 19, 24, 33–5, 46–8, 61, 64, 66, 68, 87, 117, 119
container, 9, 11, 20, 23, 61, 70, 116
coriander, 52, 55
courgette, 50–8, 61, 63, 102
cranberries, 43
cress, 45, 47, 49, 51, 53, 55, 57, 59–60, 62–5, 67, 97
crop rotation, 15–16, 61, 80
cucamelons, 27
cucumber, 26–7, 32, 41, 43, 47, 49, 51, 53, 55–7, 60, 80, 96–7
cucumber beetles, 80

120   GROW YOUR OWN FOOD

cucurbits, 56
cuttings, 30–6, 68, 77
cutworm, 74

damson, 107
Department for Environment, Food and Rural Affairs (DEFRA), 110, 114
dibber, 33–4
digging, 12, 19–20, 46–7, 60, 90, 115
dill, 51–2, 55–6, 59
diseases, 40, 56, 70, 77, 114–15, 118
division, 32, 36
drainage, 11, 15, 35
drupe, 43

eggs, 7, 110–12, 115–17, 119
eggs pest, 54, 72–5, 77–9, 81
endives, 51–2, 55–6, 59, 97

fennel, 52, 98
fertiliser, 57, 60, 88
figs, 35, 44
foraging, 104
fork, 19, 46, 48, 63, 98, 103
frost, 10, 35, 46, 48, 51, 54, 63–6, 89, 98–103, 107
fruit, 10, 12–15, 18, 28–9, 35, 37, 40, 42–4, 47–50, 52, 54–61, 63–4, 66, 68, 74, 78, 80–1, 83, 85, 88, 91, 94–5, 98–9, 102, 105–107
fungal, 60–1
fungicide, 14, 61, 81

garlic, 32, 38, 64–6, 71, 75, 98, 108
  see also, wild garlic
globe artichoke, 65, 98
gloves, 18, 61, 82–3, 108
gooseberry, 48, 50, 57
gooseberry sawfly, 77
grafting, 32, 36
grapevines, 48, 61
green manures, 15, 88–9
greenfly, 59, 68

hazelnut, 44, 108
herbs, 7, 9, 20, 52, 58, 60, 63, 65

hesperirdium, 43
hoe/hoeing, 12, 21, 53, 54, 61
horseradish, 98

iron, 40, 42
iron phosphate, 83

Japanese bulb onions, 60
Jerusalem artichoke, 98

kale, 40, 46, 48, 50, 52–4, 56, 58, 60, 63–7, 72, 74
kohl rabi, 39

lavender, 35
layering, 32, 36, 52
leaf, 21, 36, 47, 80, 96, 98–9
  leaf fungi, 71
  leaf salad, 48–9, 51, 57, 60
  leaf spot, 80
  leaf vegetables, 39–40
leatherjackets, 75
leek, 32, 38, 45, 47–8, 50–1, 53, 55, 57, 75, 98
legumes, 15, 43–4, 89
lemon, 43, 46
lemongrass, 48, 50, 52, 54, 56, 58
lettuce, 32, 40, 46, 48–50, 52–5, 57, 59–60, 62–7, 99
lime soil, 17
lime, 27, 61, 105
lopper, 22

magnesium, 40, 42
mange tout, 65, 99
manures, 15, 46, 48, 52, 60, 64, 66, 87–9
marjoram, 63
marrow, 51, 53–5
mealybugs, 71
melon, 51–2, 54, 56, 58
microclimate, 15, 52
micro-organisms, 15
mint, 48–53, 55–8, 63
mulch, 17, 19, 24, 52, 66, 70, 80, 87–9
mustard, 48, 50, 52, 54, 56, 58, 73, 89–90, 99

INDEX 121

nectarine, 46
netting, 55–6, 58, 63, 114
nitrogen, 15, 89–90
nuts, 44, 104–105, 108

onion, 32, 38, 46–8, 50–60, 62–4, 66–7, 71, 99, 102
onion fly, 75

pak choi, 50, 52, 54, 56, 58–9, 63
parsley, 32, 47–53, 55, 57, 63, 73
parsnip, 47–51, 53, 55, 57, 73, 99
path, 69, 86
pea, 16, 32, 42, 44–5, 50–5, 57, 65, 67, 89, 99
peach, 46, 63
pear, 49, 78
peat moss, 32
perennial, 89, 102, 105
peppers, 32, 43, 47, 49–53, 55–8, 60, 71, 79, 92, 100
pests, 9, 16, 29, 52, 54–6, 59, 68–70, 73–4, 77–8, 83–5, 87, 105, 114–15
plot, 12, 16–17, 66–7
polytunnel, 12–14
pome, 43
potatoes, 7, 11, 32, 39, 46–8, 50–1, 53–4, 56, 58, 60–1, 63–4, 80, 100
    see also, sweet potatoes
pots, 7, 9, 14, 33–5, 45, 50, 61, 65–6, 70, 77, 87
potting, 9, 31, 33–4, 68
propagation, 7, 30, 32, 35–7
pruning, 60, 85, 101
    pruning shears, 20
pumpkins, 51, 55, 100

radish, 32, 39, 48, 50, 52–4, 56–60, 62, 64, 66, 74, 100
rain, 17, 23, 47, 61, 83, 85, 89, 114
raised beds, 10–11, 50, 66, 84
rake, 21, 89
raspberries, 43, 47, 56, 58, 61, 63–4, 68, 101
rats, 115
red spider mite, 68
redcurrants, 35, 43, 47, 58, 68, 101
rhubarb, 32, 39, 47–8, 52, 54, 56, 58, 68, 102
rocket, 53
roots, 32–3, 35, 37–9, 47, 52, 58, 61, 63–4, 66, 68, 75–6, 80, 84–5, 87–8, 89, 96–101, 103

rooting mediums, 30–1, 34, 36
root vegetables, 38
rosehip, 106
rosemary, 35, 54
runner beans, 46, 50, 52–8, 60, 94
rust, 24

sage, 48, 50, 52, 54, 56, 58
salad leaves, 48–9, 51, 53, 55, 57, 64
sandy soil, 15, 17, 32, 90
sawfly gooseberry, 77
secateurs, 20
seedlings, 18, 30, 50, 52–3, 55, 77, 85, 94
seed trays, 48, 67
seeds, 7, 16, 19, 25–9, 32, 35, 37, 40–1, 43–5, 47–8, 51, 53, 60, 62, 65–7, 83, 86–7, 89, 94, 96–7, 99, 107
shallots, 45, 48, 50, 52, 54, 56, 58, 63, 75, 102
sloes, 106
slugs, 50, 81–3
soil, 8, 10–19, 21, 24, 29, 31, 35, 39, 46–53, 60–1, 63, 66, 70, 73–6, 78–81, 85–90, 95, 98–9, 102, 114, 117–18
sorrel, 102
spade, 19–20, 103
spider mites, 78
spinach, 32, 40, 46, 48–50, 52–4, 56–9, 62, 64, 66, 102, 108
sprayers, 73, 77–8
squashes, 14, 32, 48, 50–2, 54–6, 58, 80, 102–103
squash bugs, 79
stems, 20, 32, 34–6, 38–9, 47, 52–4, 58, 60, 71, 73–4, 80, 84–5, 88, 94–5, 98–100, 103
strawberries, 43, 48, 50, 52, 54, 56, 58, 87, 103
swede, 53–4, 74, 103
sweet potatoes, 32, 39, 47–8, 80, 103
sweet chestnut, 108
sweetcorn, 7, 50, 52–4, 56, 58, 94
swiss chard, 96

tarragon, 48, 50, 52, 54, 56, 58
temperature, 12–13, 16–17, 48–9, 55–6, 66, 71, 95, 103
thrips, 77
thyme, 290
tomatoes, 28, 32, 41, 43, 46–51, 53, 55–7, 60, 63, 79–80, 84–5, 92, 103
tomato hornworm caterpillars, 79
tools, 17–19, 46, 80

trowel, 11, 20
tubers, 38, 48, 56, 61, 98, 100, 103
turnip, 32, 39, 46, 51–2, 55–6, 59, 63, 66, 74

Vegetables, 6–7, 9–17, 21, 29, 32, 37–41, 44, 46, 48–9, 51, 53–5, 57, 60, 62–7, 69, 71, 73, 74, 77, 81, 83–8, 92–3, 97

walnut, 108
wasps, 63

water butts, 45
watering, 23, 33, 57–8, 63, 70, 73–5
watering can, 23
watering wand, 23
weeds, 12, 15–16, 20–1, 54, 61, 86–9
wheelbarrow, 10, 24, 69
whitefly, 59, 68, 80
wild garlic, 105
wilt, 57, 80, 89, 96
wireworm, 79, 80